JESUS
THE MIRACLE WORKER

What kind of
POWER
is this?

Ray Markham

AUTUMN

HOUSE

EDITOR: David Marshall, BA, PhD
READERS: Andrea Luxton, Nan Tucker,
Verna Anderson, R. J. B. Willis,
R. H. Surridge

All quotations from the Zondervan New
International Version, unless otherwise stated.
Other versions, abbreviated:
KJV – King James Version
NIV – New International Version

First published in 2001

British Library Cataloguing in Publication Data.
A catalogue record for this book is available
from the British Library.

ISBN 1 873796 92 7

Published by
AUTUMN HOUSE
Alma Park, Grantham, Lincolnshire, England, NG31 9SL

2 4 6 8 10 9 7 5 3 1

DEDICATION

To my wife Sheila, and my mother Dora,
in appreciation of their unfailing love,
support and prayers.

PREFACE

This book attempts to provide a devotional study guide to the miracles of Jesus. It is written in an imaginative style that is easy to read and understand. At the same time it presents a thorough and thought-provoking analysis of the narratives. It seeks to apply to everyday life the encouragement and challenges that these incidents bring.

I have included information about the background and context of these miracles, along with basic teaching and explanation, for the benefit of those who may be reading them for the first time. At the same time, I have sought to provide the more mature Christian with much to reflect on, not only stemming from the narratives themselves, but also from the many interesting issues they raise. Many references for further study are given, and these are brought together in Appendix 2. I also had in mind leaders of small groups, who are looking for something to guide them through the miracles and to stimulate discussion about them, without a great deal of preparatory work needing to be done.

The best way to use this book is to take one miracle at a time, first of all reading the relevant passage(s) about it as indicated at the head of each chapter, preferably in the New International Version, which is the one referred to unless otherwise stated. Then the chapter in the book can be read with the Bible account alongside for easy reference.

If readers find that this book helps to bring the miracles to life for them and draws them closer to Jesus, while at the same time enabling them to see how the teaching derived from them can be put into practice, then I shall be delighted to have succeeded in what I set out to do.

My thanks go to all those at Bretton Baptist church and elsewhere who encouraged me and gave such helpful feedback, particularly my wife Sheila. I should also like to thank Noel Jones of The Leprosy Mission for suggesting that I should write this book, and Ian Coffey for writing the foreword.

RAY MARKHAM
December 2000

FOREWORD

Have you ever been afraid of the dark?

One small boy insisted on going to sleep with his bedroom light switched on and his parents were gently encouraging him to break the habit.

'There's nothing to be scared of,' they assured him. 'Even when the light goes off, God is here looking after you.'

'That's no good,' he told them tearfully. 'I don't want God – I want someone with skin on!'

In his memorable introduction to his account of Jesus, John writes:

'The Word became flesh and made his dwelling among us' (John 1:14).

In Jesus Christ the invisible God was made visible. In every sense He is the down-to-earth God.

Ray Markham has taken each of the miracles of Jesus recorded in the gospels which reveal His power over impossible situations. But Ray provides more than a history lesson. In clear and concise language he explains what we can learn today about the transforming power of Jesus. Each study is rich in insights about discipleship and learning to grow stronger in faith. The miracles of Jesus are helpfully grouped into four sections which remind us of His power over nature, illness, evil and death.

And if, like me, you face a few mountains that look too big to climb, it's good to be reminded of the One who controlled nature, healed the sick, drove out demons and brought the dead back to life.

I have enjoyed reading these practical studies that have challenged me to take a fresh 'now and then' look at Jesus.

His power now is the same as it was then.

REVD IAN COFFEY
Senior Minister
City Baptist Church
Plymouth
September 2000

CONTENTS

INTRODUCTION

Miracles

Miracles show the power of Jesus, and are a proof of His divinity. They are evidence that the Kingdom of God has arrived. They are the Kingdom of God in action. They provide us with a glimpse of what the Kingdom of God will be like when it is revealed in all its fullness. In that day, there will be a new heaven and a new earth, with no more illness, no more evil, and no more death *(Revelation 21:1-5)*.

Rather than looking at the miracles in chronological order, I have grouped them into four sections, according to type. However, I have tried to preserve the correct sequence of events within each section. A list of the miracles covered in this book in probable chronological order is given in Appendix 1.

Looking at the miracles in this way enables us to appreciate the extent and range of Jesus' supernatural power in each area, and to compare and contrast the different incidents that fall within that particular category.

The four sections are:

- Power over nature
- Power over illness
- Power over evil
- Power over death

Faith

Throughout this book, the word 'faith' is used on a number of occasions. Perhaps, therefore, an explanation of the term before we proceed any further might be helpful.

The writer of *Hebrews* describes faith in this way: *'Now faith is being sure of what we hope for and certain of what we do not see' (11:1)*. In other words, faith says two things simultaneously. These are: I believe with all my heart that God is able to do this; and I do not doubt in my heart that God will do this. Jesus Himself mentioned these two interdependent parts when talking about faith *(Mark 11:22, 23)*.

Faith is an action word: it is something that needs to be exercised and put into practice. As the epistle of *James* says: *'faith by itself, if it is not accompanied by action, is dead' (2:17)*. Trust and obedience are often involved in faith's being outworked. Trust is where we surrender ourselves entirely into someone else's hands. Obedience is where we submit ourselves completely to someone else's will and commands.

Perhaps three examples will serve as illustrations of the points I have made.

• Imagine two people, one standing directly behind the other. The person in front is asked if he believes that the person standing behind him is able to catch him. Next he is asked if he doesn't doubt for a moment that the person behind will, in fact, catch him. Then he is asked to trust the catcher entirely by obeying the command to fall back into his or her arms. This is faith in action. Doing this confirms his faith, which, hopefully, is rewarded by his being safely caught.

• Imagine going to the doctor's. The very act of sitting in a germ-filled, crowded, noisy waiting room is proof enough of our belief that the doctor is able to diagnose the problem, and that without doubt he or she will do so when the time comes.

We then trust the doctor to the extent of doing anything he or she requires of us, however bizarre or even unseemly that might be, in the undoubting belief that this will definitely result in a successful diagnosis being made.

We further trust the doctor to list the correct medication in the appropriate strength on a prescription that before computerization was virtually illegible, and still now remains for the most part unintelligible. We even trust the chemist to mix the medicine in the prescribed amounts using the actual listed constituents.

Now comes the action part as we obey instructions and swallow the wretched stuff three times a day, in the undoubting belief that it will alleviate the problem.

• In the nineteenth century, the most famous tightrope

walker of them all was a Frenchman whose stage name was Blondin. Perhaps his most renowned act was walking across a tightrope above the foaming Niagara Falls.

One day he asked the expectant crowd which had gathered if they thought he could walk the tightrope while pushing a wheelbarrow along the rope in front of him. The excited throng readily affirmed their certain belief that he could, indeed, perform this feat. Blondin then asked for a volunteer to sit in the wheelbarrow. There was a stunned silence as no one dared even to cough or sneeze in case that be taken as an offer. Needless to say, no volunteer came forward, as no one was prepared to put his faith into action. What an experience they all missed as a result!

SECTION ONE

POWER OVER NATURE

CHAPTER ONE

DIVINE WINE

[Jesus turns water into wine]
John 2:1-11

A wedding celebration

According to *John*, this was the first miracle that Jesus performed, and it took place not on some great occasion in the capital city of Jerusalem in the presence of a great crowd, but at a wedding in Cana, a small town not far from Nazareth. We don't know for sure how weddings were conducted in Palestine at the time of Jesus, but we do know that the wedding banquet was very important, and sometimes lasted for more than a week!

Some people have the mistaken idea that Jesus was a bit of a killjoy. If that were so, He'd hardly have been invited to such a joyful occasion in the first place. He obviously felt quite at home at such an event. Indeed, He even used weddings as teaching points: consider the parables of *The Wedding Banquet* (*Matthew 22:1-14*), *The Ten Virgins/Bridesmaids* (*Matthew 25:1-13*), and *The Wedding Feast* (*Luke 12:35-40*).

It is often difficult to decide whether to accept invitations to certain social events, and the example set here by Jesus is very helpful. On the one hand, as we have seen, He was not a killjoy; but on the other hand it would be difficult to imagine Jesus getting drunk – or behaving in such a way that gave the lie to what He taught, or caused Him regret the next day.

Such occasions often provide opportunities for witness, so it makes sense to approach them with that in mind, while asking

God to create openings for us, and praying that we might use them with wisdom and boldness.

Telling Jesus

The ceremony over, the guests all get stuck into the food and drink. After a while, a rumour begins to circulate, and reaches the ears of Mary, the mother of Jesus. The unthinkable has happened. They have run out of wine. There could be nothing more embarrassing for the bridegroom than this. It was his responsibility to provide more than enough food and wine, or face the disgrace of being seen to lack hospitality. The shame of this is hard for us to imagine.

Mary finds Jesus, and tells Him *'"They have no more wine"' (3)*. At this point, she is probably hoping that Jesus might somehow be able to get hold of some from somewhere to save the blushes of their host. Whatever her thinking was, the point is that she told Jesus about the problem, although, of course, He already knew.

There is an important principle here. Although God already knows what we need *(Matthew 6:8)*, He waits for us to bring our needs to Him. This shows our Father that we mean business with Him, and we want Him to become involved. We are handing the situation over to Him: taking it out of our hands and placing it into His. God expects us to tell Him about our perils *(Matthew 8:25)*, our questions *(Matthew 24:3)*, our sicknesses *(Mark 1:30)*, our difficulties *(Mark 6:35, 36)*, our needs *(Mark 10:51)*, our failures *(Mark 9:28)*, our family troubles *(Luke 9:38)*, our disappointments *(Luke 24:21)*, and our bereavements *(John 11:21)*, knowing that He is there to meet us at the point of our need, when we ask Him to.

Leave it to me

When Mary tells Him about the problem, He responds firmly, but gently. The Greek word translated *'Dear'* in verse 4 was a term of respect and endearment. *'"Why do you involve me?"'* He asks her. *The Amplified Bible* renders this *'"What is that to you and to Me?"'* and then adds by way of clarification of the Greek used here: *["What have we in common? Leave it to Me"'].* Which presumably is why, in verse 5, Mary says to the servants, *'"Do whatever He tells you"'.* But more of that later.

Mary's solution reflects human thinking with all its limitations, which has nothing in common with the way Jesus sees it. He knows that there is no more wine available anywhere in the quantities required. The only solution is a supernatural one, and that's why He says, *'"Leave it to me"'.*

Jesus goes on to say: *'"My time has not yet come"'.* He has come to fulfil a particular mission, which is to die on the cross. All the events of His life are leading towards this moment, when truly His *time* will have *come.* That is His focus. But throughout His ministry we see His compassion for people in need compelling Him to involve Himself in situations which are not fundamental to His mission. Clearly, Mary has understood from their conversation that Jesus is actually going to do something about the situation, and she realizes that it may well involve some rather unexpected instructions; and that's why she says what she does to the servants in verse five.

Sometimes it may seem that God is not really interested in our problems, because, although we've told Him about them, nothing much seems to be happening. Be assured that God is at work, but in His way, and in His time. Leaving it to Him may result in unexpected things starting to happen in our lives to bring about God's solution to the problems, and it's often during such times that our faith in Him is really put to the test. So often when we bring problems to God in prayer, we have our own fixed ideas of how He will solve them, just as Mary probably had. What a wonderful privilege we have of bringing God's supernatural, all-seeing and all-knowing perspective to bear on the situation. It's this leaving-it-to-Him that we so often find difficult.

The answer lies in the jars

Each of these six stone water jars held twenty to thirty

gallons *(6)*. If my maths is correct, that's between 120 and 180 gallons in total. I don't know about you, but I can't visualize that amount, so I think of it like this. The average car holds about ten gallons of petrol. So, imagine going to the petrol station and filling more than twelve cars to capacity, and then you have some idea of the quantities involved here.

You may wonder what those jars were doing there in the first place. They certainly weren't put there in case Jesus might want to use them to perform a miracle! *John* tells us that they were *'the kind used by the Jews for ceremonial washing' (6)*. This was when water was poured over their hands to cleanse them from anything that had caused them to become defiled during the course of the day: for example, having contact with Gentiles.

There is another important principle here. God often uses what is already in our lives and circumstances to bring about His solution. It may be people, possessions, events; anything. We often expect God to cause something to come into our lives, when the answer is actually in the jars over there.

The servants obeyed Jesus' command to *"'Fill the jars with water"'*, and fill them *"'to the brim"' (7)*. So far, no problem, except that the servants probably thought there was going to be an awful lot of cleansing going on. It's what Jesus said next that must have got their minds racing overtime. *"'Now draw some out and take it to the master of the banquet"' (8)*. I can just imagine those servants standing there, open-mouthed, looking at one another, gasping in disbelief, wondering if they had heard correctly. They were being asked to take samples of water to the master of ceremonies to taste as if they were wine? The consequences didn't bear thinking about. At the very least the master of ceremonies was going to think they were winding him up, and his anger at being mocked like this could well result in their dismissal from service. And yet, wasn't there something different about this man Jesus? People just seemed to do as He told them to. Hadn't His disciples left everything and followed Him when He told them to? And His mother seemed to have every confidence in Him. Hadn't she said, *"'Do whatever he tells you"'*?

So they did as Jesus had instructed. I just wonder if they could resist sneaking a look to see if the water had changed colour at all, or taking a sniff in the hope of smelling the bouquet of wine.

In my experience, it's relatively easy to obey God when we're not being asked to do anything that we find difficult. The crunch comes when God tells us to do something we're not all that keen on doing, or we don't understand the reason for. It is at this crisis of faith that our obedience and submission to God's ways are really tested. At such times, it's important to remind ourselves that it is our loving, caring Father who is at work, and that we can have every confidence in Him, as the servants came to have in Jesus. Taking encouragement from the faith and example of others, as the servants did from Mary, will help, although we may still have doubts, and wish we could sneak a look at the water or smell it to see if it's changed.

Choice wine

What would the master of ceremonies' verdict be? It is important to notice that although the servants knew the source of this new wine the master of ceremonies did not (9). So his judgement on it was bound to be impartial, made solely on the quality of what he was tasting, and not being influenced either way by knowing that Jesus was in some way involved. He was so staggered at this wine's quality, that *'he called the bridegroom aside' (9c)* to explain to him, privately, that it was usual to bring out the best wine first, while the guests were still sober enough to appreciate how fine it was; not leave it till later, when they might be incapable of such judgement *(10)!*

Well, what could the bridegroom say? Obviously, nothing! To admit that he had no idea where this batch of wine had come from would be to confess to his not providing sufficient hospitality. So he wisely kept quiet.

Of all the wine that was provided that day, this batch was described by the master of ceremonies as *'"the choice wine"' (10);* top quality vintage. And Jesus provided an abundance of it. Up to 180 gallons of wine had just been produced, yet it tasted as though it had gone through all the wine-making processes.

When God pours out His blessing upon His people, it is the best thing that can be experienced, and there is plenty of it. God is never impoverished through giving. He has an abundant supply of blessing; and what He provides is always top quality.

I don't know how long it was before the master of ceremonies and the bridegroom found out about the source of this choice wine. Perhaps they became followers of Jesus as a result; we don't know. What we do know is that this miracle and other *'miraculous signs' (11),* as *John* describes them, were fundamental to the disciples' coming to *'put their faith in him' (11).* They saw, and believed. Which reminds me of Jesus' words to Thomas after the Resurrection, words also recorded in *John (20:29):* *' "Blessed are those who have not seen, and yet have believed." '*

CHAPTER TWO

THERE MUST BE A CATCH

[The miraculous catch of fish]
Luke 5:4-11

Twofold command

Luke tells us that such a large crowd has gathered on the
seashore to hear what Jesus has to say, that He has had to use
Simon's boat as a makeshift pulpit from which to talk to them
all. In fact, the design of the pulpit in many old churches is based
on the stern of such a boat.

Simon is washing his nets after fishing all night when Jesus
asks for his help *(2, 3)*. Jesus finishes speaking to the crowd, and
turns to Simon with these words: *'"Put out [launch out: AV] into
deep water, and let down the nets for a catch"' (4)*.

Notice that Jesus' command to Simon is twofold, with the
second part being dependent on the first part being obeyed. He
cannot *let down the nets for a catch* unless he has first of all *put out
into deep water.*

It is often the case that other prior steps have to be taken
before the final goal, outcome, or answer to prayer can be
effected or arrived at. Sometimes, we wonder why nothing
seems to be happening, be it in our personal lives or in the life of
our church. Maybe it's because God has told us to do something,
or even not to do something, and we still haven't obeyed; and
that's why God cannot take us on to the next step. If you find
yourself in such a situation, remind yourself of what God last
said to you or to your church, and then prayerfully consider

whether this has been obeyed. Being obedient to God is fundamental to seeing Him at work. If Simon had not obeyed, there would have been no miracle.

Getting into deep water

There were several reasons I put off as long as possible learning to swim, and one of them was that I didn't relish the thought of getting out of my depth. It was a very real fear that I had to conquer. I felt safe in the shallow end; my feet touched the bottom; I was in full control of what was happening, and I wasn't scared that I might drown at any moment! It was quite fun splashing around there, and I felt secure. But I wasn't making any progress, and I wasn't experiencing anything new. I certainly wasn't using the swimming pool for the purpose for which it was really designed.

It was only when I had the courage to launch out from the side into the deep water that I started to find out what it was like to swim. Slowly but surely I began to experience what it was like to move in a whole new dimension. It was exhilarating. And, as I became more confident, I began to wonder why I had allowed my fears to hinder me for so long.

Simon's boat can be seen as representing you and me. God designed us to sail, not to be moored. He fashioned us to experience the deep water, not to stay in the shallows of the port. Clearly, a boat cannot sail to its full potential in the harbour. It needs to be out on the sea to do that. If we want new experiences in God, are we prepared to leave the security of the shallows and to set sail for the deep, where we allow ourselves to be led and moved by the winds and currents of the Holy Spirit? If we are, then we can begin to fulfil our potential in God, and experience the exhilaration of the moving of the Spirit in our lives. We are no longer in control. He is. And then we'll begin to wonder why we let our fears hold us back for so long.

There has to be a desire on our part to launch out. God won't push us out into deep water if we don't want to go there. Unlike Simon's boat, we do have a brake!

Launching out requires faith in God, a faith that is prepared to trust and obey as we enter the unknown, and begin to sail in previously uncharted waters. Hearing what God is saying, and talking to Him about what's going on, become even more important.

Simon's boat can also represent our church or fellowship. Jesus built it to sail and to bring back treasures for Him. In my experience, there are always people in the boat who would much rather stay safely in the shallows, enjoying the peacefulness of the port, and that's understandable. But the fish are in the deep, not in the harbour.

God longs for us to launch out into the community around us, and not just to stay safely in the security of our buildings. This means being prepared to cut loose the ropes that keep us bound, and raise the anchor that keeps us stuck where we've always been, and set sail to make an impact for Christ.

As we launch out, there are five important questions to consider. First of all, are we being sensitive to the winds and currents of the Spirit, which are always moving, flowing, changing? Sailing against these winds and currents will get us absolutely nowhere.

Secondly, are we prepared to take directions and instructions from the Captain of the boat and from those God has placed in leadership over us? Our support for them in prayer is vital as they seek to hear from God and be aware of the needs of their motley crew.

Thirdly, do we have a unity of purpose? Of course, we shall all still have our different tasks to perform while sharing a common purpose – to ensure that the boat is sailing smoothly and efficiently at all times.

Fourthly, are we pulling together? Imagine what would happen in a boat where the crew were all trying to pull in different directions! All they would end up doing would be to go round and round in circles! Unfortunately, this is an all-too-familiar sight in too many churches.

Fifthly, is everyone pulling his weight on the oars? There is no room for slackers; this just puts added pressure and responsibility onto others, who, sooner or later, will collapse under the strain. Unfortunately, in my experience, 80% of the work in a church is usually done by 20% of the people, who are totally exhausted as a result. No wonder the boat doesn't make the progress it should! It is only due to the remarkable commitment of this dedicated minority that it makes any progress at all. I just wonder what the Boat-builder thinks about this.

The 3 Rs

Now we come to the second part of Jesus' twofold command to Simon. Having *put out into deep water,* he is to *let down the nets for a catch.*

Jesus knows Simon has had a disastrous night's fishing before he even mentions it, and out of compassion for him He wants to help in the most practical way possible. Jesus does care about our everyday needs and the routine of our lives, and He wants to meet with us right here in the midst of our daily activities. We often think that some of the things that trouble us are too small or mundane for God to bother about, but it is often here that God wants to reveal Himself to us.

• *Reaction*

I can just imagine the expression on Simon's face as he replies: *"'Master, we've worked hard all night and haven't caught anything'" (5a).* I can see the colour draining from his face and a look of tired despair clouding his features. I can hear the disillusioned weariness in his voice. He is probably off home for a meal and a sleep after he's finished washing the nets, and here is Jesus telling him to go back out there and try again. I imagine that if it was anybody but Jesus, he would have a few stronger words to say!

But, in spite of how he's feeling, he responds to the fact that it's the Master speaking to him, even though he's probably thinking to himself that it can't possibly be that simple; there must be a catch somewhere. Little does he know! So, in spite of his doubts, he says to Jesus: ' "But because you say so, I will let down the nets" ' (5b). The Amplified Bible renders it: 'But on the ground of Your word, I will lower the nets [again].' We can always act on the solid foundation of the Word of God, and put our complete trust in it.

I'm sure we can all identify with the feeling of toiling all night and catching nothing. Many Christians have laboured faithfully and unceasingly through the years, seeking with limited success to win men and women for Christ. It's not that they've been doing anything wrong, any more than Simon and his fellow fishermen had. In fact, it would have been exactly the same nets that Simon used when he went out at Jesus' command as he had previously used during the night. The difference was that the second time they were acting under Jesus' direct instructions and perfect timing, and the result was an incredible, miraculous catch of fish.

Simon normally experienced varying degrees of success when he went fishing; and so will we when we go fishing. Sometimes there will be little evident response as we share the Gospel. But there will also be times when God seems specially to bless and anoint our efforts, or gives the Church a specific Word about what to do at a specific time. Listening to God, who is the One who provides the catch, is vital, as is being ready to act in faith in response to what He says, in spite of how we may be feeling at the time. And that means making sure we are always 'in deep water' where the fish are.

• *Reward*

When we step out in faith in response to God's Word, there is always a reward. Simon's faith was rewarded by a catch that contained *'such a large number of fish that their nets began to break'* (6). God always honours faith in Him; and a willingness to do things His way and in His time always brings results.

The reward was so great that it touched the lives of others not directly involved *(7)*, and drew them into what God was doing. This often happens when God moves in a miraculous way. People who are on the fringe of things are drawn into the work of God, with the result that their relationship with Him deepens and grows.

There is another side to this. Just imagine the amount of work that this enormous catch required of Simon and his fellow fishermen! All these fish would have to be sorted, cleaned, gutted and sold. I'm sure we should all love to see tens of thousands if not millions of people accepting Christ as their Saviour and Lord and coming into the churches. But we need to appreciate that a great deal of follow-up work would need to be done. All these people with their different problems, circumstances, needs, hang-ups, difficulties, etc, all needing to be sorted. A wonderful situation to be in, I agree! But a situation that brings with it a tremendous responsibility that would need to be shared by everyone in the churches, not just a few.

• *Response*

Now we come to a very moving scene. Simon is on his knees before Jesus, presumably in the boat, with all these fish teeming around him, saying, *'"Go away from me, Lord; I am a sinful man!"'* *(8)* This is his response to being in the presence of the One who has caused something miraculous to happen, leaving them all totally *'astonished' (9)*. Simon's brash self-confidence has been replaced by humility and the dawning of an understanding of the awesomeness of God. He has been brought to a point of recognizing his own unworthiness before God. Perhaps for the first time he is seeing himself as God sees him, and his response is to submit himself to the Lordship of Christ in his life.

It's only in God's presence that we see ourselves as we really are: sinful, rebellious people, who need to repent and submit themselves to God. It's wonderful to know that when we do this we are always assured of His love, mercy and forgiveness, whatever we may have done.

It was only when Simon was humble and yielded that he could be used. And so it is with us. God longs to use us to our full potential and bring to pass what He has planned for us, but this can happen only when we are prepared to allow Him to have His way completely and unreservedly in our lives. It was only then that Jesus encouraged Simon and revealed what He had planned for him. '"*Don't be afraid; from now on you will catch men*"' (10b). And He has the same plan for us.

A price to pay

But there was a price to be paid; and Simon knew it, and so did James and John. *Luke* tells us: '*So they pulled their boats up on shore, left everything and followed him*' (11). They literally left everything: the boat, which was their livelihood; the fish that they had just caught, which could have made them wealthy; the business, which they had built up – especially James and John Zebedee who employed others *(Mark 1:20)*; the culture of the Galilean fishermen, which had formed their values, attitudes and language; their families, whom they loved, and their friends, whose camaraderie they valued; the safe, ordered life of the fishing community, which had given them a certain security. All this they were now exchanging for an uncertain, unpredictable existence as disciples of this man from Nazareth.

Following Jesus demands full commitment on our part. There is a cost to discipleship, which we have to weigh up *(Luke 14:25-35)*. Jesus made it clear that it has to be our number-one priority, and it has to come before everyone and everything else in our lives *(Matthew 6:33)*. It may not mean full-time service in the minister/missionary sense, but being a disciple is still a full-time calling for each one of us.

Some years ago, I wrote a song called '*I would your disciple be*', the words of which I think are appropriate here.

Shine your light into my life, O Lord,
Help me to see what you see;
I don't want to be just a convert, Lord,
I would your disciple be.

In your life and in your death, O Lord,
You were committed to me;
I am overwhelmed by your love, O Lord,
I would your disciple be.

Lord, I give myself into your hands,
Take me and fashion me;
Lord, make me a vessel that you can use,
I would your disciple be.

Set my heart on fire for you, O Lord,
Kindle the flame within me;
Fill me with your love and power, O Lord,
I would your disciple be.
Be glorified in me,
Let your Spirit flow through me,
Be enthroned in me.

CHAPTER THREE

ALL IN THE SAME BOAT

[Jesus calms the storm]
Mark 4:35-41
(also Matthew 8:23-27; Luke 8:22-25)

Introduction

Of all the nature miracles recorded in the gospels, this is the one, as far as I'm concerned, which shows in the most dramatic way that Jesus is Lord of all creation.

"'Let's go over to the other side'"

Mark tells us in verse 35 that Jesus said this to His disciples *'when evening came'*. But why did He say it? Perhaps it was simply so that He could get away from the crowds who had been following Him all day. The three accounts of this miracle have different events preceding it; but, whichever one you look at, it's clear that Jesus had been heavily involved in teaching and heal- ing. And, as we'll see later, He was completely exhausted by all this ministry. So, He was intent on *'leaving the crowd behind'* (36).

And sometimes in our own lives God would have us leave the crowd behind, and just be in the boat with Jesus, where He is the only focus of our attention. There we leave behind on the shore all the crowds of things that would distract us from concentrating fully on Him, and we begin to sail with Him; and, as a result, we learn more about Him.

Or perhaps it was because Jesus knew that across the other side of that lake was a man who desperately needed Him: a Gentile, whose healing would cause a tremendous stir in that region, foreshadow His ultimate victory over Satan, and bring many people to God [see chapter 15].

Whenever God speaks to us, either individually or as a church, we can be absolutely certain that He's done it for a purpose, and that for us He has something amazing in store, which will bring glory to His name.

Why the 'squall' was 'furious'

As a child, I used to wonder mischievously what had made this *'squall'* so *'furious' (37)*. Had somebody upset it? That was until I found out the real reason why such violent storms suddenly blow up on the Sea of Galilee, even out of a clear blue sky. Apparently, it's all to do with the fact that the Sea of Galilee is situated in a basin 212 metres below sea level and surrounded by mountains. What happens is that cool air from the Mediterranean Sea gets sucked down through the passes in these mountains and clashes with the hot, humid air that generally lies over the lake.

I'm not sure that the disciples possessed such a thorough knowledge of the cause of these climatic conditions; they just experienced the frightening results. The fishermen among them would have coped with such conditions many times before, which just goes to show that this particular storm must have been a real belter. The Amplified Bible translates it as *'a furious storm of wind [of hurricane proportions]'. Mark* tells us that *'the waves broke over the boat, so that it was nearly swamped' (37)*. It was so bad that these experienced fishermen just couldn't cope with this storm. It was above and beyond anything they'd faced in the whole of their lives, and their attempts to handle the situation were failing absolutely.

I can just picture the disciples trying desperately to control the boat, furiously baling out water in a valiant attempt to prevent the boat from sinking, and generally getting into a complete and utter panic as the situation just went from bad to worse.

And where was Jesus while all this mayhem was taking

place? What was His contribution to saving the boat and its inhabitants from impending disaster? *Mark* supplies us with the answer. *'Jesus was in the stern, sleeping on a cushion' (38a).* What a lovely picture that conjures up. There was Jesus, totally exhausted by the day's events, fast asleep with His head on the leather cushion that was kept under the coxswain's seat, seemingly completely oblivious to the drama that was happening in the boat. Here we glimpse His humanity, before we witness His deity.

Desperate people

I expect the disciples were thinking that Jesus was bound to wake up any minute. But He didn't, and things were going from bad to worse. They had reached the limitations of their human abilities in attempting to deal with the situation. They couldn't think what else to do. Everything they had tried in their own strength or as a result of their own thinking had been totally unsuccessful and had completely failed to provide a solution to the problem they were facing. They were absolutely desperate and at the end of their tether.

Someone once said: 'Man's extremity is God's opportunity.' God responds to desperate people. Like me, do you ever find yourself behaving rather like the disciples? They were rushing around, trying to sort out the problem in their own strength and by their own thinking, when all the time the Problem Solver was fast asleep at the back of the boat. They had to come to the point of acknowledging their impotence in the situation before Jesus was able to do anything for them. And the same applies to us. So often we struggle on for so long trying to cope with the circumstances we're in, trying to sort them out for ourselves, instead of handing them over to the One who has the answer. And that's the key: actually handing our problems over to Jesus, because He won't just appear and take over uninvited; that's not God's way. He waits patiently until we get to that point where we realize that we desperately need Him, and we cry out to Him from the depths of our soul. And then He responds.

I'm sure Jesus was fully aware of all that was happening, even though He was asleep. He was just waiting for them to call on Him. And call on Him they did; rather bluntly and insensitively, in fact. *Mark* tells us: *'The disciples woke him and said to him, "Teacher, don't you care if we drown?"'* *(38b)*. Of course He cared. He'd been caring all the time He was seemingly just asleep. He was just waiting for them to give Him the opportunity to show how much He cared. He was there, in the boat with them, just waiting to be asked.

In my experience, there are times in my life when it seems as though God is asleep. You often hear people say: 'God doesn't really care', and 'Where was God when I needed Him?' The answer is that He was there in the boat with you, caring about what was happening to you, and just waiting for you to hand the situation over to Him.

The Christian life is never going to be storm-free. In fact, Jesus promised us the opposite, saying: *"'In this world you will have trouble"'* *(John 16:33)*. That's all part of living in a fallen world. God doesn't shield us from the storms when we become His disciples, otherwise people would become Christians for the wrong reason: to avoid having storms in their lives. Rather, He wants to use our storms to reveal Himself and His power to us, so that they become faith-provoking rather than fear-inducing experiences.

He let them go through it

If Jesus had wanted to He could have spared the disciples this experience. With His divine knowledge, He could have said, 'We won't cross over the lake just yet. There's going to be the most awful storm. We'll wait an hour or so, and then we'll go.' But He didn't. He let them go through it, because He wanted to teach them some very important principles that they would remember and build on in the future.

Jesus wanted to teach His disciples what to do when faced with the situations they would encounter years ahead. When those times came, they would be in charge of sailing a boat called the Church; facing the storms of persecution, whose waves would threaten to swamp the Church and sink it without trace. This actually happened as the gospel writers were committing the events of Jesus' life and ministry to manuscript so that they would be passed on to future generations and not die with them. For me, it becomes very poignant as I imagine *Matthew, Mark* and *Luke* coming to write up this miracle, and remembering that just as Jesus was with the disciples in the boat all those years ago, He was present with them in the Church, and present with them individually as they were persecuted, and, in some cases, martyred for their faith. What comfort and reassurance the account of this miracle must have brought them as they recited it to one another in those dark and stormy times!

God allows us to go through the storms, whatever form they may take, and whatever the final outcome, to enable us to experience the reality of His presence with us as we call out to Him in faith.

'Be muzzled!'

Jesus knew exactly what to do in this situation, as He always did in every situation that faced Him. *Mark* tells us that *'He got up, rebuked the wind and said to the waves, "Quiet! Be still!"'* *(39a)* The sense of the original Greek here is *'Be muzzled!',* which for me always conjures up a picture of a dog that has been dealt with in this effective way for barking or biting once too often. Both the bark and the bite of this storm have been muzzled by the Lord of Creation. And the result is that *'the wind died down and it was completely calm' (39b).*

Apparently, although wind can just die down in a moment, waves cannot suddenly become calm: there is always a time factor involved. Yet here we see that when the Lord of the waves speaks the laws of nature are suspended; they respond to their Creator, and there is an immediate calm.

When they saw this, I wonder if any of the disciples recalled the words which they would have known from the *Psalms: 'You rule over the surging sea; when its waves mount up, you still them'* (89:9). Or: *'Then they cried out to the Lord in their trouble, and he brought them out of their distress. He stilled the storm to a whisper; the waves of the sea were hushed'* (107:28, 29).

I often find that it's in times of storm that words of Scripture come into my mind, and I derive great strength, encouragement and comfort from them.

The peace of God

The word *'Quiet!'* or *'Peace!'* is just as important. Like the muzzled dog, the storm can no longer disturb or upset. Jesus wants to bring you His peace in the midst of your storm. Let me remind you of His wonderful words: *' "Peace I leave with you; my peace I give you. I do not give to you as the world gives. Do not let your heart be troubled and do not be afraid" '* (John 14:27).

There is an important difference between the peace that *the world gives* and the peace that God gives. And it's simply this: the peace that the world gives depends on the situation, whereas the peace that God gives does not. The peace of the world depends on there being an absence of turmoil; the peace of God is ours when we are in the midst of turmoil. That's how we know that it's God's peace: because it's not natural to experience peace when you're in a crisis; panic is more usual!

I'd known the truth of this for years, but it was only recently that I actually experienced the peace of God in my own life. I badly dislocated my left elbow playing indoor football. It was so bad that everyone went quiet; I could put the fingers of my right hand into the socket where the elbow should be. When the staff at Casualty saw it, they went into a corner and muttered to one another, and then one of them told me that it was wonderful what they could do with elbows these days. Thanks! Just what I wanted to hear. I lay there awaiting treatment, convinced I would need operations and goodness knows what else; and yet I had this overwhelming sense of peace, and I knew it was from God. He was there, present with me in my storm, to such an extent that the storm just didn't exist any more. It had been muzzled, and all I could feel was the peace of God. The wind had died down, and it was completely calm. Or, as *The Amplified Bible* puts it *'there was . . . a great calm (a perfect peacefulness)"' (Mark 4:39).*

I can assure you that I have achieved no great heights of sanctification, spirituality or saintliness. I include this incident only to glorify God and to testify to the truth of His peace being given in times of turmoil. In the end, having X-rayed my disaster, they managed to manipulate it back into place. Before they did so, they gave me a full dose of morphine, telling me that this would make me feel good. I didn't feel any different. It must have been because I was so full of the peace of God that I was feeling good already!

It was only some days later that I found out that the casualty staff had called me 'the unfazed patient'. Apparently, this was because they were totally amazed at how I just seemed to take everything they told me or did to me in my stride, with no fear or panic. Nothing seemed to faze me, according to them. I was humbled by the thought that they had seen the peace of God at work in my life.

Fear or faith?

Now that calm has been restored, Jesus turns to His disciples and asks, *'"Why are you so afraid? Do you still have no faith?"' (40).* I don't think Jesus is angry with them; more exasperated by their lack of faith.

This is Jesus' recurring frustration with the disciples throughout His ministry. It's almost as if He is asking them what else He has to do to bring them to a point where they just automatically have faith in Him, even in times of trouble.

I'm sure we frustrate Christ in just the same way. So often we fail to have faith in our God as we should, in spite of all He has done. I don't know about you, but I often find myself crying out to God because of fear, rather than faith. The disciples were scared to death they were going to drown. Was it the fright that made them wake Him? Or did they believe that He was able to do something miraculous to change the situation? Both *Matthew (8:25)* and *Luke (8:24)* have the disciples crying out, *'"Lord, save us! We are going to drown"' (NIV).*

Here we see another example of God's amazing grace. When the disciples woke Jesus, He didn't say that He wasn't prepared to do anything about the storm because they may have asked out of fear rather than out of faith. They'd asked, and that was sufficient for Him to respond and to act immediately, because He had compassion for them. It was when the problem had been dealt with that He got them to reflect on the root cause of their cry. God wants us so to walk with Him in faith day by day that He becomes our first port of call in a storm, rather than our last.

Paul says that *'We live by faith, not by sight' (2 Corinthians 5:7).* In other words, we must look at Jesus, whom we can't see, and not at the storm, which we can see, believing that He is Lord of all. To complete the verse from *John* that I quoted earlier: *'"But take heart! I have overcome the world"' (16:33c). The world,* which is the source of many of the storms that blow up in our lives, has been *overcome,* just as surely as the storm on the Sea of Galilee was overcome.

Simultaneous emotions

The accounts of this miracle mention a dual reaction from the disciples to what they had just witnessed: the simultaneous emotions of fear and amazement. Rather than falling on their knees in gratitude, which we might have expected, *Mark* tells us that *'They were terrified' (41a).* They were more afraid of the power that had stilled the storm than they were of the storm itself. In fact, this kind of reaction can be seen several times in The Old Testament. When God did something spectacular, the people were often frightened: for example, at Mount Sinai (See *Exodus 20).*

The disciples' fear expressed itself in the rhetorical question, *'"Who is this?"' (41b).* They were coming to terms with the fact that they had seen God in action in the flesh in this dramatic way. Then their amazement took over. *'"Even the wind and the waves obey him"'* (41c). Together they were trying to grasp the reality of what had happened before their very eyes.

It is fitting that we show reverence when we are in the presence of the Almighty God, who can do miraculous and amazing wonders. In the words of the apostle Paul: *'Now to him who is able to do immeasurably more than all we ask or imagine, according to his power that is at work within us, to him be glory in the church and in Christ Jesus throughout all generations, for ever and ever! Amen!'* (Ephesians 3:20-21).

CHAPTER FOUR

MULTIPLICATION AND DIVISION

[The feeding of the 5,000]
Matthew 14:13-21; Mark 6:30-44; Luke 9:10-17;
John 6:1-13.

The disciples

I have always found it interesting that this miracle is the only one that can be found recorded in all four gospels. Considering the number of miracles Jesus performed, I am rather surprised; it shows us just how important and significant this event was.

Mark and *Luke* tell us that the twelve disciples have recently been sent out by Jesus in pairs to *'preach the kingdom of God and to heal the sick' (Luke 9:2)*. They've done this with great success *(9:6)*. The question is, will they be able to apply what they've learnt to other situations in the future? The teaching profession calls this 'transfer of training'. Now they've been schooled in the work of the Kingdom, will the disciples be able to transfer their training to the situation they are about to meet?

Notice Jesus' thoughtfulness towards His disciples here. He listens to them as they excitedly pour out all the details of what has happened on their tours, and I'm sure His heart was thrilled by it all; but knowing how exhausting such hands-on experiences can be, He is just as concerned for them to get some rest *(Mark 6:31)*, so He gets them all into a boat, and they set off together across the Sea of Galilee in the direction of Bethsaida.

Compassion

I can just imagine the reaction of the disciples as they near the shore of the Lake and see crowds of people waiting for them, or, more accurately, waiting for Jesus. The inward groans and outward expressions of despair and frustration. Or perhaps I do them an injustice to think that they might have reacted as I would have.

How differently Jesus reacted. *Matthew (14:14)* and *Mark (6:34)* both speak of His *'compassion',* a word which so beautifully describes His dealings with people who came to Him with seeking hearts throughout His earthly ministry. Compassion is more than just loving care and concern, more than just pity. It is all of those, but it is far more. It always involves action, as clearly set out by Jesus in the parable of *The Good Samaritan (Luke 10:25-37)*. His shepherd heart was stirred, and He responded by talking to them and healing those who were sick.

The crowd

Let's consider this crowd for a moment. Why had they followed Him? Why did they want to be in His presence so desperately? What were their reasons? *John* is quite blunt about it: *'because they saw the miraculous signs he had performed on the sick' (6:2)*. I imagine four groups of people, each of which reacted to seeing Jesus' working in power in a different way, and were therefore part of this huge welcoming party for quite distinct and different reasons.

• The first group had been drawn by the *prospect of seeing more of the spectacular*. It was 'the Jesus show', and they wanted the best seats! They were probably wondering whatever this 'magician' would do next. They had come to be entertained, and they didn't want to miss anything.

• The second group were drawn purely by *curiosity*. They were quite content to watch proceedings from a distance without actually getting involved. They had probably responded merely intellectually to what they had seen Jesus do, and were hoping to find some logical explanation for it all.

• The third group had simply *misunderstood.* They thought Jesus was only about meeting their physical needs, and they wanted to take advantage of what they saw as being on offer. Their attitude was probably underpinned by the sentiment: 'I want what I can get out of God, but that's as far as it goes'. (We'll deal with the fourth group separately.)

All the people in these three groups would go away unfulfilled and disappointed, because they had come to Jesus for the wrong reasons. What a tragedy! And yet, how often are we guilty of making the same mistakes? How often do we come into God's presence for the wrong reasons and out of wrong motives? It's so easy to do this.

• Like the first group, we can find ourselves coming just to see signs and wonders. There's nothing wrong with wanting to see God at work in mighty power, and I praise Him for the times I have experienced this. But that should not be my prime purpose for entering His presence; if it is, then I need to re-examine my motives. Signs should follow Christians, but too often Christians follow signs.

• So often we can fall into the second group, being content to watch from a distance without committing ourselves to God in the way that we should. Unfortunately, many Christians seem content to stay on the fringe, rather than involve themselves in the life, worship and family of the church. Both the church and especially the individual concerned are impoverished as a result. An intellectual curiosity can be healthy, provided it brings us ultimately into a relationship with Christ. However, it is important to remember that no one ever comes to this point through intellect alone, as the ways and mind of God are past our understanding. Faith, not intellect, is the starting point for knowing God.

• Like the third group, we may fall into the trap of misunderstanding what Jesus is about. We live in an age which seems to encourage the self-centred attitude, and we can find ourselves treating God a bit like a vending machine as a result. You put in your request, and out pops the answer, just like a chocolate bar. Some people seem to think that God exists to meet their needs, not to mention their wants. Their love for God seems to depend on whether or not He answers their prayers at once. Now there are times when God does graciously respond to our requests immediately, but in my experience they are the exceptions rather than the rule. Jesus' love for me is unconditional, and that makes me realize that my love for Him should also be without conditions, to the point where I can truthfully say that if God never ever answers any more of my prayers for the rest of my life, that will in no way affect my wholehearted love for Him.

So what about the fourth group in the crowd? These were the people who just wanted to meet Jesus. They were seeking. They had high expectations. They realized that they needed His touch upon their lives. They recognized something different about Jesus. He was no ordinary prophet; His miraculous powers proved that. They realized that He was the Messiah, the Son of God, and they wanted to meet with Him in a real way. If this is our reason for coming to Jesus, then He will meet with us. Can you imagine the difference it would make in our personal lives and the life of our church if every time we came into the presence of Jesus we had seeking hearts, high expectations, were willing for our lives to be changed, and realized that we were coming into the presence of the Son of God, for whom nothing is impossible? It would certainly transform many of our meetings, not to mention our lives.

The mountainside

Notice that *John* sets this miracle on a mountainside *(6:3)*. He did this quite deliberately, because the Jews appreciated the significance and symbolism of the mountain.

• It was a place of communication. It was at Mount Sinai that God had communicated His requirements to His people through Moses; their special relationship had been confirmed, and the Covenant had been sealed *(Exodus 20)*. According to Matthew's gospel, Jesus gave His great sermon on a mountainside to emphasize the fact that His teaching was taking over from that previously given by Moses. The time was right for God to come in the flesh and communicate with mankind directly. It was also a place where He went to communicate with God in prayer and to develop His own personal relationship with God. Jesus frequently withdrew to such a place during His ministry, as we shall see in chapter 5.

• The mountain was a place of revelation, where God showed Himself in glory. This had already happened at Sinai. Peter, James and John would shortly experience this amazing phenomenon for themselves on what has become known as the Mount of Transfiguration. On that occasion, the glory of the Son of God was displayed before them as Jesus spoke with Moses [representing the Law] and Elijah [representing the Prophets], followed by a further communication from above. (See *Matthew 17; Mark 9; Luke 9.*)

• It was also a place of demonstration, where God showed His awesome power. Again, Sinai is an obvious example; but perhaps the best example is Mount Carmel *(1 Kings 18)*, where Elijah called on God to demonstrate to the prophets of Baal that He was the one true God, after which you could say that things got a little fiery, and too hot for the Baal worshippers to handle!

Coming to the mountainside is symbolic of coming into the presence of God. The mountainside is where we hear from God, learn about God, and see God in action. The crowd has come, expectantly, to the mountainside, and something supernatural is going to happen. Every time we come together, expectantly, into God's presence, we, too, are on the mountainside, and something supernatural will happen. If I want supernatural things to happen in my situation and circumstances, then I need to come to the mountainside and wait upon the Lord.

Let's begin to look now at the events of this miracle as they unfold before us. *Matthew, Mark* and *Luke* tell us that the crowd were with Jesus in this remote place for most of the day, and that it was getting late. The disciples urged Jesus to send the people away so that they could buy themselves something to eat. I'm sure the local villagers and farming folk would have been thrilled to bits having five-thousand-plus people descending on them trying to buy food! Can you just imagine the amount that would have been required to send all these men, women and children away with full stomachs? Mercifully for them, Jesus didn't see the locals as providing the solution to the imminent food crisis. The answer was closer at hand.

I particularly like John's account of what happens next, because he makes the conversation between Jesus and His disciples much more personal. His response to the disciples' urging is to turn to them and ask: *'"Where shall we buy bread for these people to eat?"' (5)* Notice the lovely way in which Jesus includes Himself in the question. I think this is very significant, and I wonder what response Jesus was looking for when He asked that question. From the way He phrased it, He seemed to be wondering whether the disciples were still looking at situations from a human perspective, or whether they were at last able to transfer what He had taught them to the problem of feeding five thousand people.

What reply do you think would have gladdened the heart of Jesus, and would have made Him think that He was actually making some progress with this motley crew He had assembled? I think it would have been something like: 'We don't need to buy bread. You can do it, Lord. Nothing is impossible for you. We have experienced your provision while we've been on the road, and we believe that you can provide for these people. We can't see how you can possibly do it, but we know that you can do the miraculous!' I reckon that such a faith response would have made the spirit of Jesus jump for joy at the realization that at last His disciples were beginning to understand who He was and what He was teaching them. Such joy was, in fact, at least one more miracle away.

Jesus seems to be looking to Philip in particular to answer the question. Philip, who always looked at things from an intellectual, logical, even mathematical point of view. Philip, the one with the local knowledge, coming as he did from the nearby town of Bethsaida, and so should have a good idea where they could get food. 'Well, Phil, what shall we do?' True to form, Philip looks at the situation intellectually and mathematically, and, like all good mathematicians, he comes to a conclusion, which goes something like this: 'It's impossible to do anything, Lord, because, according to my calculations, it would take over two hundred denarii [which, if I could just remind you, is equivalent to eight months' wages for the average working man these days] to give them even a bite to eat, and we just don't have that kind of cash in hand. So my advice is, forget it!' Philip's solution to the problem is to ignore it, but the problem still remains. His negative response gives Jesus nothing to work with.

Now it looks as though Andrew might be going to say something. Andrew, who always looked at things from a practical and realistic point if view. 'What about it then, Andy? What shall we do?' It strikes me that Andrew is probably rather embarrassed and maybe a little tongue-tied at this point, as he shepherds a boy with five loaves and two fish towards Jesus. Now of course we'd all like to know where the boy got these provisions. The fact that we're not told means that it's not the least bit important, but nevertheless it is fascinating! Most likely his mother had packed him up a huge lunch and tea. 'Well, you know how these boys eat and eat.' And this is what is left over. If that is the case, it seems to me he would have needed a donkey to get it all there in the first place! I like to think that he was sent by his father – an enterprising local farmer, who had heard about the problem, or perhaps had already had hungry people calling at his farm – to sell bread and fish to the crowd, thus making a nice profit for himself. However the loaves and fish come to be there, Andrew sees them as a contribution to the solution. He sees that, looking at the situation practically and realistically, they can't possibly be the solution. Or can they? At least Andrew's faltering response gives Jesus something to work with.

But what about *our* response? We all face difficult, even impossible situations in our lives, and, when we do, is our response any different from that of Philip or Andrew? The vast majority of the miracle accounts in the gospels teach us a very clear lesson, and it is this: the problem is not the situation; the problem is our response to the situation.

So, do we tend to respond in a negative, even dismissive way as Philip did, turning to God and saying: 'It's impossible; don't even bother!' Or are we more like Andrew, saying things like: 'I can't see how you're going to do it, God, but I've really got no choice but to turn to you, believing that you can do something'? I have to admit that too often this kind of faltering, wavering response is the one I find myself making. What does encourage me is that this is usually the disciples' response as well, and look what they went on to do! At least it gives Jesus something to work with, and perhaps more importantly, to work *on,* to bring me to the point where my response is full of faith, when I turn to God and say: 'Lord, I believe you are the God of the impossible, and I put all my faith and trust in you.'

Perhaps that's the point *John* is emphasizing by mentioning the boy in his account, which the other writers don't. Throughout his ministry, Jesus used children as examples of pure, unquestioning faith, the kind of faith on which the Kingdom of God is built, and continues to be built today.

As we look at the circumstances we are in at the moment, perhaps we need to ask ourselves this searching question: Am I part of the solution, or am I part of the problem? In other words, are my wrong attitudes and wrong responses preventing God from working out the answer to this situation? But let's also encourage our hearts in the knowledge that there is no problem that is impossible for God to solve; no need that is too great for

God to meet; no situation that is beyond the power of God to deal with. And my response to that is simply to say: 'Praise the Lord!' When we put our faith and trust in God, miracles happen.

Resources

I think what happens next is another marvellous example of the graciousness of God. Jesus takes what Andrew has given Him in response to His question, and uses it to perform a miracle. I'm sure He didn't need five loaves and two fish in order to provide miraculously for this throng; He could just as easily have fed them from nothing, in the same way that He had brought the whole of creation into being. But clearly Jesus had purposed to use that which already existed in order to perform this miracle, and thereby to teach His disciples, and us, about what can happen when we submit what we have to Him.

There seem to be four parts to this miracle, which we can identify more easily if we follow *Mark's* account at this point.

• *The submitting*

The disciples submitted the five loaves and two fish to Jesus. Now, these loaves were actually barley loaves, the food of the poor, not loaves made of wheat. But Jesus didn't despise what He had been given, and refuse to use it on the grounds that it wasn't up to standard. He took what had been submitted to Him. I find that so encouraging and uplifting. However inadequate our resources may seem to be, the Master will still accept them, if we submit them to Him, and place them into His hands.

This applies to us as churches, and also as individuals. In my experience, there are some Christians who feel that the gifts and abilities they have are too limited or insignificant for God to use. Let me encourage you by saying that whatever talents you possess, many or few, they have been given to you by God to be used in His service; but, for them to be fully effective, you must submit them to Him. The reason for this will become clear as we go on.

- *The blessing*

The first part of verse 41 reads: *'Taking the five loaves and two fish and looking up to heaven, he gave thanks and broke the loaves.'* Before meals, Jews would always thank God for the food and ask His blessing and anointing upon it. In the same way, when we submit our resources to the Master, He will put His blessing and anointing upon them. This will make all the difference to their effectiveness and the impact that they will have.

- *The returning*

That same verse continues: *'Then he gave them to his disciples to set before the people.'* Those same barley loaves and fish are returned to the disciples to divide among the crowd. It would have been no good if the disciples had just stood there, totally amazed at what was happening, and not given the food to the people. God gives to us, not to impress us, but so that we can give to others.

It's also interesting to note that Jesus did not change in any way what He was given to bless. He was given barley loaves, and He returned barley loaves; He didn't change them into wheat ones. God doesn't change the talents and abilities He has given us, because to do so would be to change us from how He made us into different people. He returns to us what He originally gave to us, which we in turn have submitted to Him for His blessing and anointing.

- *The multiplying*

And it is only as we use the resources that the miracle takes place. The fact that they now have God's blessing and anointing upon them makes them far more powerful and effective in the furtherance of God's Kingdom than they would have been if used only in our own strength. God takes and multiplies what we give Him, for His glory.

Abundance

And what a multiplication we see here. *'They all ate and were satisfied'! (42)* All five-thousand-plus of them. It must have taken ages to distribute the food. Now that's what I call long division. There were even twelve baskets full of scraps left over at the end. Some 'remainder'!

God is a God of abundance. Jesus didn't just provide them with a snack. He wanted them to eat their fill. God wants to fill us with his love, His joy, His peace, His forgiveness, His power, His strength, and whatever else we need to receive from Him, not just give us a taste of it. God wants us to experience Him in all His fullness, and not to be satisfied with bite-size chunks, as we often are.

Old Testament echoes

There are some other points in these accounts that Jewish Christians would have particularly noticed as they read them, beside the significance of the mountainside.

• One is the way Jesus directed the people to sit down *'in groups of hundreds and fifties' (Mark 6:40)*. This would have reminded them of the order of the camp in the desert at the time of Moses.

• Another is the fact that food was provided in a place described as *'solitary'* by *Mark* and *'remote'* by *Matthew* and *Luke*. This would have reminded them of the provision of manna at the time of Moses in another solitary, remote place – the wilderness. One rabbi had said: 'The first redeemer (Moses) made food come down from heaven. The last redeemer (the Messiah) will too.' What a great confirmation this miracle would have been to them that Jesus truly was their long-awaited Messiah and Redeemer, especially as they were enduring a great deal of persecution at this time at the hands of Jews who had rejected Jesus as the Messiah.

• A third point they would have found significant is that according to *John* this miracle occurred at the time of year when *'The Jewish Passover Feast was near' (6:4)*. Passover was, and still is, the time to remember how God had brought about their salvation from the Egyptians under the leadership of Moses. The blood of lambs had been shed in order to cover the Jewish people from the judgement of God upon the land of Egypt. At the very next Passover meal, Jesus, already identified by John the Baptist as '"the Lamb of God who takes away the sin of the world"' (John 1:29), 'took bread, gave thanks and broke it, and gave it to them, saying, "This is my body given for you; do this in remembrance of me"' (Luke 22:19).

The events of this meal, which became known as The Last Supper, are clearly foreshadowed here, with Jesus breaking the bread [His body] and distributing it to the people, with more than enough to meet the needs of everyone.

• They would also have noticed that in *John's* account Jesus said to His disciples: '"Gather the pieces that are left over. Let nothing be wasted"' (6:12). Jews regarded bread as a gift from God, and so, if you dropped any scraps of bread during a meal, you had to be sure to pick them up. That's why bread was seen as a powerful symbol of the Word of God, given to feed us spiritually; hence Jesus' subsequent teaching about Himself being 'the Bread of Life'. So this whole event is symbolic of the Jews' being fed by Jesus' teaching. However, this feeding is not for the Jews alone; it is also for non-Jews, a point illustrated by the fact that Jesus miraculously fed four thousand people while in Gentile territory (Matthew 15:32-39; Mark 8:1-13).

Whenever God's word is given out, it is never wasted. Let's be encouraged by that, because I'm sure there are times when we do wonder if the faithful giving out of God's word, in whatever way it is done, is actually achieving anything. Let's remember the words of the writer of *Ecclesiastes*: 'Cast your bread upon the waters, for after many days you will find it again' (11:1).

Temptation

Bread also features in the first of the three temptations that Jesus experienced. (Matthew 4:1-4.) Having been challenged by the devil to turn stones into bread, Jesus replied by quoting from Deuteronomy 8:3: 'Man does not live on bread alone but on every word that comes from the mouth of the Lord.' Satan assumed that Jesus would be tempted to take this route to popularity by using His powers to give bread to the hungry multitudes of His day. But Jesus has not come primarily to meet man's physical needs; it is spiritual food He has come to bring, which is far more essential to man's well-being.

I'm sure Jesus would have recalled the devil's mocking words as He saw the hungry crowd before Him that day, and plenty of available stones. So why did He apparently go back on His decision? The answer lies in that word 'compassion', which came up right at the start of these events, and throughout His ministry. He was not going back on His earlier decision at all. He provided for them purely because His compassionate heart went out to them in their extremity. He certainly didn't make a habit of it; on only two occasions did He feed the crowd during the whole of His ministry.

Persecution

To the first Christians reading these accounts, the fish, which usually get only a fleeting mention in any analysis of this miracle, would have been significant too. They were living during a time of persecution by the Romans, and so had to meet secretly. Because their lives were in danger, they needed a sign by which they could recognize fellow believers, and the fish was the sign they used.

This had nothing to do with the fact that some of the twelve disciples were fishermen; it had to do with the Greek language. At that time, everybody spoke two languages: their native tongue and Greek, which had become the international language, eventually to be superseded by Latin. In Greek, the word for fish is 'ichthus'. The letters of this word were taken as an acrostic for **I**esous **C**hristos **T**heou **U**ios **S**oter, meaning: Jesus Christ, of God, the Son, Saviour. This formed an early statement of faith about who Jesus was, which they all shared, and so the fish became the symbol of that belief and the sign of its acceptance. To them, the events of this miracle would have been a total vindication of their faith in Jesus as being the

Christ/Messiah, the Son of God, the Saviour. And so it is for us as well.

Obedience and submission

John makes a significant statement about Jesus' distributing the bread and fish *(6:11)*. He says: *'Jesus . . . distributed to those who were seated as much as they wanted.'* There are two things to notice here.

• First of all, Jesus ministered only to those who had obeyed Him by sitting down as He had directed them to do. Presumably, those who were standing up didn't get any. If we want God to impact our lives, then we must do as He says, and submit ourselves to Him, even though we may not always understand the reasons for His directions at the time. Those who obeyed Him were focused on Him, and less likely to be distracted by what else might be going on around them. Consider the difference there would be if we made God the focus of our lives too, and were less concerned about what others might be doing or saying.

• Secondly, Jesus respected the wishes of each individual. God never overrides our free will; He never forces Himself on us. None of the crowd was force-fed! They could have gone away hungry and empty if they'd wanted to, but that was not what Jesus wanted. He had made abundant provision for them all, if they wanted it. We, too, can go away from God's presence hungry and empty, and, tragically, we sometimes allow that to happen. But that's never what God wants. He wants us to enjoy His abundant provision for us, both when we meet together as His people and in our daily walk with Him. The question for us to consider is: 'How much of God do I want in my life?', because that's the amount we'll get.

CHAPTER FIVE

DO YOU SEE WHAT I SEA?

[Jesus walks on the water]
Matthew 14:22, 33; Mark 6:45-52; John 6:16-21

Preparing to pray

This miracle takes place straight after the feeding of the 5,000; the same night, to be precise. It is early evening by now, and Jesus gives the disciples clear instructions to get back into the boat and set sail across the lake, known both as Lake Genneserat and the Sea of Galilee, for Bethsaida. Presumably He intends to meet up with them there the next day. Jesus Himself dismisses the crowd, rather than leaving it to the disciples, so that the people are in no doubt that His teaching and miracles are at an end for the day, otherwise they will probably stick around all night, not wanting to miss anything.

Jesus must have been longing for some time on His own after such a hectic day, and He is determined to get some uninterrupted peace and quiet so that He can pray. Notice how he *'went up on a mountainside' (Matthew 14:23),* the place of communication with God, as we saw in chapter 4. The gospels tell us that Jesus deliberately set aside time to pray to the Father on a regular basis. Jesus also commanded us to pray, so it must be important. You may well accept that; but if my experience is anything to go by, it's quite another matter actually to do it. For a start, I have no mountainside within easy access, even if I had the time or the energy to climb up it. But what I see here are two important principles: making a time to pray, and making a place to pray.

Jesus was certainly a very busy person, with so many demands on Him every day of His ministry. So busy was He that He had to make a time to pray; He had to organize His life to make sure that communion with His Father did not get squeezed out of the day, as could so easily have happened. Here we see Him quite deliberately sending the disciples off in such a way that they couldn't possibly come and interrupt Him, and then sending the crowd off in such a way that they were in no doubt that there was no point in hanging around any more that day.

Although our situations are obviously completely different from that of Jesus, the same principle applies. It is important that somewhere in the routine of each day we make a time to pray. I find that I have to plan it deliberately, otherwise it just doesn't happen. And I try to make it quality time, not when I'm going to be totally exhausted or about to drop off to sleep. I don't pretend that this will be easy for you, particularly if you have a young family, but even if it's just five minutes, you'll find it will become the most precious and important five minutes of your day.

Jesus made a place to pray. He was in such public demand that it often had to be a lonely place, otherwise He would be seen, and the crowds would come flocking. Most of us don't have that problem, although we may still feel in demand. It is just as important for us to make a place to pray. It might be on the journey to work, as we go to the shops, come back from taking the children to school, take the dog for a walk, do the washing up, hang out the washing, or prepare the meal. It can be on the bus, on the train, in the kitchen, in the garden, in the car, in the woods, in the lounge, in the garage, in fact anywhere. But it's our place, and our time, when we commune with our Father God. And we have to organize it and make it happen, as surely as we have to with all the other important things in our daily lives.

Help is at hand

Meanwhile, back on the lake. It's now *'the fourth watch of the night' (Matthew 14:25),* which on our clock will be somewhere between three and six in the morning. The disciples are in trouble in the boat, due to the strength of the wind and the mounting waves. *Mark* tells us that Jesus *'saw the disciples straining at the oars, because the wind was against them' (6:48a)*. Jesus knows that although the fishermen among them have encountered similar conditions on the lake many times before, on this occasion they are going to be in real difficulty. So we read that *'Jesus went out to them, walking on the lake' (Matthew 14:25)*. *John* tells us: *'When they had rowed three or three and a half miles, they saw Jesus approaching the boat walking on the water' (6:19a)*. So Jesus must have walked some distance on the sea to reach them.

This shows us that just praying for people, though very important, is not enough; we must be prepared to offer them practical help. Jesus left His time and place of prayer specifically to offer His disciples practical help. Jesus never leaves us to struggle on our own in the circumstances which beset us. There are times when we can feel quite alone, trying desperately to deal with the situation, and feeling as though we are getting nowhere; a bit like rowing into a headwind. It is at these times that Jesus is unfailingly there, walking across the waves of our conflict, walking resolutely through the winds of our adversity, to offer us the help we need at the very moment that we need it the most. And He does it because He loves us, just as He loved the disciples in that boat.

Here we see another example of Jesus' performing the miraculous, purely out of divine compassion for people, never for His own self-glorification. I can't imagine anyone else who could walk on water actually doing it at three o'clock in the morning, when the lakeside was totally deserted, and, in any case, visibility was probably poor, and it was dark. We'd be much more likely to do it at three o'clock in the afternoon, when everyone could see, and probably sell people tickets to watch this amazing spectacle! As far as we know, Jesus only ever walked on the water once, and it was done solely in response to the need of His disciples at the time.

The disciples' reaction

And how do these disciples react when they see this figure walking across the waves in their direction? Do they shout out with joy and relief that it is Jesus come to save them from their situation? All three accounts give us the same answer. They all 'cried out' all right! But not because they were overjoyed; rather 'because they all saw him and were terrified' (Mark 6:49, 50). It's interesting that they realized something supernatural was happening, but they jumped to the wrong conclusion. Mark tells us that 'they thought he was a ghost' (6:49). They interpreted what they saw within the framework of what they as humans were able to believe.

It's easy to be critical of the disciples here, and say that they should have recognized Jesus. Well, perhaps they should have, but as far as they were concerned, He had gone off somewhere to pray, and they didn't know where. They didn't know He could see them (6:48), let alone that He was able to walk on water. In their panic they misunderstood what was happening.

How easy it is for us to do the same! When we find ourselves in difficulties, God can sometimes seem to be a long way off; remote from what we are going through. It's as though He's on the land, while we're on the sea. Yet we are never out of His sight; His eyes are always upon us. There is nothing that happens to us that He does not know all about, even before it has happened. Nothing takes God by surprise! I wonder how many times He 'appears' in our lives, and we don't even realize that it is God. In our panic, we don't recognize Him. We may even think that this can't possibly be God, but it is all the time.

Amazing love and amazing grace

Notice that Jesus has not appeared on the scene in response to the cries of the disciples. He has come right where they are because He has seen the trouble they are in, and His compassion has brought Him there. And sometimes we can be so taken up with our circumstances that we even forget to pray about them, and yet God sees us, loves us, and comes to us. What amazing love that is!

Which takes me back to an interesting sentence that you will find only in *Mark*. It comes at the end of *verse 48*, and reads: *'He was about to pass by them'*. Jesus had come right where they were, but the next move was up to them. Jesus never gets into our boat without our permission. What amazing grace that is! That I can actually reject the help of the One who can change the situation I am in if I so wish, and He will abide by my decision. Why is that? Simply because God never overrides our free will to choose, and wants us to hand over the situation to Him willingly. He waits for us to cry out to Him, and then He will get into our boat, and we can expect a miracle.

'I AM!'

Notice how Jesus' response to their cries was immediate. In *Matthew* we read: *'But Jesus immediately said to them: "Take courage! It is I! Don't be afraid"'* (14:27). There will be times when we need to be courageous and fearless, because God may require us to take certain courses of action that either may not be easy, or are not what we want to do, or for which we don't understand the reason. But once we invite God into the boat, we must be obedient to what He tells us.

Our courage and confidence should stem from the fact that it is God Himself, the all-knowing, all-seeing, all-powerful one, who has come to us. Jesus says to them: *'It is I! Don't be afraid.'* This can also be translated: *'Fear not! I AM!'* The same God who had announced Himself as *'I AM'* to Moses at the burning bush *(Exodus 3:14)* was there present with them in Jesus at their point of need. *'I AM'* is a powerful present reality, who is at work now, right at this moment. Throughout the Old Testament we read that God said: *'I am the God of Abraham, of Isaac and of Jacob'*, not I *was*. The same power of God that we see at work in the Bible is at work today in the lives of those who are willing to invite Him into their boat.

The boat is also a symbol of the Church, so we can see

further meaning here. It is, in fact, possible for the Founder of the Church to be excluded from it. For the One who loved the Church and gave Himself for it not to be welcome in it. Sometimes this can happen without our realizing it. It's not that we mean to shut I AM out, any more than the church at Laodicea did *(Revelation 3:14-20)*. How important it is to keep Christ at the centre of all we do, and to give the Holy Spirit the chance to move among us in power, otherwise we shall be doing just that.

Just think of the transformation there would be in the Church in this country if the Great I AM, the God of Abraham, Isaac and Jacob, the God who was in Christ walking across the water, were to be welcomed back fully into His Church, rather than being allowed to pass by. How we need the power, the wisdom and the mind of Christ in the Church today!

Peter steps out

It is at this point that Peter comes into the picture. Jesus is telling them that it's He, but the ghost idea is taking some shifting. So Peter decides to take matters into his own hands. *Matthew* tells us what happens next. *'"Lord, if it's you," Peter replied, "tell me to come to you on the water." "Come," he said' (14:28, 29a)*. Now, at that point, if I'd been Peter, I'd have probably thought: 'It must be Jesus, because He's told me to come; so there's really no need for me to get out of the boat. Instead, I'll just ask Him to get into the boat.' Not Peter! What a wonderful picture *Matthew* paints for us as he describes what happened next. *'Then Peter got down out of the boat, walked on the water and came towards Jesus. But when he saw the wind, he was afraid and, beginning to sink, cried out, "Lord, save me!" Immediately Jesus reached out his hand and caught him. "You of little faith," he said, "why did you doubt?"' (29b-31)*.

I'm always impressed by the courage and boldness that Peter shows here. He actually gets out of the boat, and steps out in faith. And it's when we show faith, and do not doubt, that miracles can happen. Peter actually walked on the water, which none of the others did. If God gives us a clear command [here it was 'Come'] that is witnessed to by others [they all heard what Jesus said to Peter], whether individually or as a church [here it was to an individual, but Jesus would have said the same to any of the others, had they asked], then it's time to exercise our faith and get out of the boat.

James tells us that *'faith . . . if it is not accompanied by action, is dead' (2:17)*. Faith is something we do, not something we believe. Peter could have believed he would walk on the water if he got out of the boat, but if he had chosen not to put his faith into action, then it would have been of no effect. In my experience, talking faith is easy, living it is not. The other disciples missed out on this amazing experience, simply because they were not prepared to get out of the boat.

God is looking for people who are prepared to get out of the boat in obedience to His command, and thereby to accomplish great things for Him through unswerving faith in the Great I AM. My prayer is: 'Lord, may we be a "water-walking" people!'

Walking by faith requires us to keep our eyes firmly fixed on Jesus, and not look at the circumstances around us. That's where Peter went wrong. He was doing so well, until he got to the *'but'*. It was when he took his eyes off Jesus, and *'saw the wind'* that *'he was afraid'*. He suddenly thought to himself, 'Whatever am I doing? You can't walk on water. It's impossible!' followed by a tremendous 'Splash!' Fear replaced faith. He doubted what he was experiencing, and lost it. The inevitable followed; he began to sink.

I'm sure many of us have experienced this. It is easy to start off well, and then get distracted by events around us from keeping our focus firmly on God. And then that sinking feeling becomes all too familiar. But be encouraged: God never gives up on us. Jesus didn't turn His back on Peter in disgust, and leave him to make the best of it. He didn't say things like: 'I don't know; he's let me down again. When will he ever learn? Serves him right. Getting soaked will teach him a lesson!' When Peter cried out, Jesus responded immediately, and pulled him up.

It's interesting what Jesus then says to him, as Peter stands there, dripping wet. I try to imagine the tone of voice He used, and the more I think about it, the more convinced I am that it was not one of rebuke but of gentleness, as if to say: 'You were doing so well; I was so proud of you. Why did you let doubt come in and spoil it? Next time, keep focused on Me all the time!'

I'm sure we often feel that we let God down, but I honestly don't think He sees it like that at all. Rather, I believe He sees it as another step in our learning curve as we walk with Him. God never rebukes us for stepping out in faith in response to His command. He wants us to learn from our experiences, and to keep on getting out of the boat.

Twofold result and twofold response

When the disciples realized that it was Jesus, John tells us: 'Then they were willing to take him into the boat' (6:21a), and the immediate result of that was twofold. Firstly, 'the wind died down' (Matthew 14:32). And so it is that whenever we bring God into the situation we experience a calm, and a peace that is divine. Secondly, 'the boat reached the shore where they were heading' (6:21b). When we bring God into the situation, we shall always find ourselves at the place where we should be, because He alone knows the complete plan He has for our lives. There are times when we veer off the course that God has ordained for us because we make the wrong choices. But God's grace is such that He will use the storms we face to blow us back on to the right course, provided we are willing.

This twofold result caused a twofold response in the hearts of all those in the boat. Mark tells us that 'They were completely amazed, for they had not understood about the loaves; their hearts were hardened' (6:52). The implication is that they shouldn't have been the least bit amazed or surprised. Only a few hours before they had witnessed Jesus' miraculous feeding of 5,000-plus people with just five loaves and two fish. Yet it seems that they had failed to grasp the significance of this: that Jesus was able to override the laws of nature whenever He chose. The fact that He could walk on water should not, then, have come as any surprise. Yet, how often are we surprised when God does something supernatural in our personal or church situation, when really we should expect it?

The other response is to be found in *Matthew*. *'Then those who were in the boat worshipped him, saying, "Truly you are the Son of God"' (14:33)*. Their amazement at what they had seen led to a realization of the One who Jesus really was, and that realization led naturally to worship. Our amazement at His sacrifice for us on the cross and at His resurrection from the dead should inspire our hearts to worship Him also, and to say with the disciples in the boat: 'Truly you are the Son of God.'

SECTION TWO

POWER OVER ILLNESS

CHAPTER SIX

TOUCHING THE UNTOUCHABLE
[A man with leprosy]
Mark 1:40-45; (also Matthew 8:2-4; Luke 5:12-14)

Leprosy: the facts

At the time of Jesus, leprosy was an incurable disease, and everybody dreaded catching it. The skin of people with leprosy became covered with the most awful sores, and the flesh withered away, drastically altering their appearance. If that wasn't bad enough, it could be as long as thirty years before the person actually died of the disease.

Social and religious consequences

There were social and religious consequences too. Because it was thought to be such a contagious disease, no one was allowed to touch a person with leprosy, and such people were not allowed to mix in society. The attitude to leprosy then was rather similar to many people's attitude to AIDS today: a combination of fear and disgust. Apparently, some people even went to the extent of throwing rocks at sufferers to stop them getting too close. They were outcasts, who often lived in colonies outside the towns and cities.

They were also regarded as being outside God's chosen people; so they not only became social outcasts, but religious outcasts as well. Touching such a person for whatever reason, made you religiously unclean, and you had to take certain prescribed steps before you were considered fit to worship God once again.

The Law of Moses, which the Jews lived by, contained clear instructions about skin diseases and rules for those who suffered from them *(Leviticus 13, 14)*. In *13:45, 46* we read: *' "The person with such an infectious disease must wear torn clothes, let his hair be unkempt, cover the lower part of his face and cry out, 'Unclean! Unclean!' As long as he has the infection he remains unclean. He must live alone; he must live outside the camp." '*

Food would sometimes be left for the leprosy sufferers outside the city walls as the gates were locked for the night. What a sad sight it must have been to see these dishevelled, disfigured outcasts approaching the city walls, squabbling over the food, and then shuffling off again into the night.

Shocking behaviour

Luke tells us that *'Jesus was in one of the towns' (5:12)* when this incident occurred. The sufferer had no business to be there, and must have known he was breaking the rules. He then compounded this by approaching Jesus without so much as an 'Unclean!' falling from his lips. Shocking behaviour indeed!

Mark tells us that the man *'came to him* [Jesus] *and begged him on his knees, "If you are willing, you can make me clean" ' (1:40)*. Here we see a man, driven by the desperation of his disease, who had heard that Jesus had *'healed many who had various diseases' (34a)*, and had the faith to believe that what He had done for others Jesus could do for him.

Desperation and faith are a powerful mixture, and they had propelled him through the social and religious restrictions of the day to the feet of Jesus, where he beseeched Him on bended knee.

As the man knelt there, he must have been fearful as to how Jesus might react to the temerity of his actions, particularly as leprosy was widely regarded as God's punishment for sin. Would this Jesus be willing to grant healing, or would He, too, reject him?

When we come to God with our needs, whatever they may be, it is important that we show similar qualities of humility and expectancy. As we come, let us remember that faith expects, but does not demand, and that healing comes within the sovereign will of God.

Shocking response

Throughout the Gospels we see that Jesus is always willing to heal those who have faith in Him. *Mark* continues his account with these three wonderful words that sum up the whole ministry of Jesus: *'Filled with compassion . . . ' (41a)*. In chapter 4 we noted that compassion always involves action, and on this occasion it provokes Jesus into a shocking response, which *Mark* describes thus: *'Jesus reached out his hand and touched the man' (41b)*.

Jesus frequently touched people to bring them healing. But in this case such an action broke the Jewish Law *and* made Jesus religiously unclean. Yet His compassion for the man in response to his faith was so great that it overcame any such considerations. Jesus was more concerned about the condition of the man than about any implications for Himself. He touched him, thus technically becoming 'unclean' so that the man might be made clean.

What a wonderful picture this is of what Jesus would do on the cross! He who was holy and sinless would become unclean for us, taking our sin upon Himself. As *Peter* puts it in his first epistle: *'He himself bore our sins in his body on the tree'* [cross] *(1 Peter 2:24a)*. And the purpose of this was that we might be made clean, cleansed from the leprosy of our sin by the blood of Jesus shed on the cross. In his first epistle, *John* tells us that: *'the blood of Jesus . . . purifies* [cleanses] *us from all sin'*, provided of course that *'we confess our sins' (1 John 1:7-9)*.

What a glorious feeling of unspeakable joy must have surged through that leprosy sufferer's whole being as he felt the gentle hand of Jesus laid upon him. There at last was someone who saw past his physical condition, and saw him as a person. There at last was someone who cared about him and accepted him, disgusting as he was. No one is too disgusting for God to touch.

It could be argued that Jesus didn't actually need to touch the man to heal him: the spoken word would have been enough. But Jesus is always concerned about the whole of us, not just our bodies. This man needed more than physical healing: he needed to feel accepted. And that was the importance of the touch.

Jesus speaks the word

The words that Jesus spoke to him must have thrilled him too: *'I am willing. . . . Be clean!' (Mark 1:41c).* Jesus was actually willing to heal him, an outcast and a reject. Could he believe it? Dare he believe it? Be clean! The words must have rung in his ears. Could it be true? The incurable cured?

I imagine the man tentatively folding back the sleeve of his cloak, scarcely daring to look at his arm; lowering his face cloth and gingerly touching the skin of his cheeks to see if it felt any different. And his joy at discovering that it did.

Mark tells us that *'Immediately the leprosy left him and he was cured' (42).* As soon as we come to God in prayer, He begins to do something in our lives and situation. Although we may not see the results immediately, His response is immediate.

The fact that the man was healed immediately after Jesus spoke the word would have been very important to people in those days. At the time, there were many Greek wonder-workers, who went around using spells, props and various rituals, claiming to heal people by means of them. This miracle shows that Jesus is not just another such wonder-worker. He does not need spells or rituals of any kind. He just speaks the word, and people are healed. And they would begin to ask themselves the question: 'Could this be the Messiah, promised to us by God?'

The Messianic secret

What Jesus says next seems rather strange and unrealistic. *Mark* tells us that *'Jesus sent him away at once with a strong warning: "See that you don't tell this to anyone"' (43, 44a).* In fact, this happens on many of the occasions when He has healed someone. It is as though Jesus wants to keep the fact that He is the Messiah a secret for the time being until the time has come for Him to reveal His true identity fully. This happens during the events of the crucifixion and resurrection, although He does reveal the secret to His disciples privately *(8:29, 30; 9:2-9)*.

Jesus could also have been concerned how the Romans might react if they were to hear talk among the Jews about the arrival of their Messiah, otherwise known as the King of the Jews. They were always on the lookout for potential threats to the stability of the Empire, such as people going round claiming to be kings. So, hearing such talk, they could have arrested Jesus prior to His ministry's being completed and before the right time had arrived for Him to make His claim. Obviously there was going to be talk about His miracles, but He wanted to keep it to a minimum for the time being.

Jesus and the Law

It is important to understand that Jesus did not go around habitually breaking the Law of Moses. On the contrary, He was loyal to the Law, except when it prevented God's will being done or a human need being met. Other miracles will provide us with further examples of this principle.

So, having warned the leprosy sufferer about not telling anyone, Jesus then instructs him to *'"Go, show yourself to the priest and offer the sacrifices that Moses commanded for your cleansing, as a testimony to them"' (1:44)*.

Jesus was referring to the procedure laid down for such eventualities in *Leviticus 14:1-32*. If a person did recover from leprosy, which was, in fact, a term that covered all kinds of skin ailments, he had to go to the priest, who would give him a thorough examination and then pronounce him clean, so that he could be accepted back into the community. He also had to offer special sacrifices.

Jesus shows His loyalty to the Law by insisting that the man follow its instructions to the letter. The sacrifices would be evidence to both the priests and the people that the cure was genuine, and would reinforce to them that Jesus was loyal to the Law.

There is another aspect to this. Jews believed that only God could cure leprosy (see the story of Naaman in 2 *Kings 5:1-14*), so this miracle would be further evidence to them of Jesus' divine power.

The challenge of transformation

As we would expect, the man finds it impossible to keep the news to himself *(45)*. His life has been totally transformed by his encounter with Jesus, and his joy at being cleansed and restored knows no bounds.

The man now faces a new challenge. He has to adapt to a completely new lifestyle. Just think for a moment of the many ways in which his life is going to change, owing to the cleansing that he has experienced. The places he goes to, the people he associates with, and the way he spends his time – all of this is going to be very different.

We, too, have experienced cleansing from the leprosy of sin, and this also brings with it the challenge of a completely new lifestyle. Perhaps this is the time to consider prayerfully the places we go to, the people we associate with, and the way we spend our time, to see whether everything is in keeping with what God wants of us.

This is not to say that we should abandon everything we have enjoyed doing or people we have enjoyed being with. But they should be able to see the transformation that has taken place within us, which will be evidenced by our new lifestyle, bringing them to the point of asking us what has happened to effect such a change.

This reminds me of the words to be found at the beginning of the book of *Psalms*: '*Blessed is the man who does not walk in the counsel of the wicked or stand in the way of sinners or sit in the seat of mockers. But his delight is in the law of the Lord, and on his law he meditates day and night. He is like a tree planted by streams of water,*

which yields its fruit in season and whose leaf does not whither.
Whatever he does prospers' (1:1-3).

The challenge of acceptance

There are other lessons to be learnt as well. I wonder how
readily the community accepted the man into their midst? I
imagine that there would have been a certain amount of suspi-
cion, reservation and caution in the air. I can just see them hud-
dling together in their little groups, pretending not to stare at
him, and asking one another in whispers whether it really was
the man they used to know and so assiduously avoid. They
knew it was, of course. They had been there when the priest
pronounced him fit to re-enter society, assuring them that a
thorough examination had taken place and that the appropriate
sacrifices had been made. And yet, knowing was one thing;
accepting was quite another.

We also have to face the same challenge as people's lives are
transformed and they are brought into the churches. The Early
Church had to face up to a particularly difficult situation in this
respect. Their chief tormentor and persecutor, a man by the
name of Saul, had an encounter with Jesus and his life was
transformed. He was on his way to round up all the Christians
who lived in Damascus when the risen Lord appeared to him on
the road as he approached the town *(Acts 9:1-9)*. God spoke to
Ananias, a member of the local church, about it *(9:10-19)*.
Ananias, for reasons he explained very strongly indeed, had
grave doubts about accepting Saul into the brotherhood of
Christians there in Damascus. But the way he was prepared to
listen to God and to bring Saul into fellowship, despite his
strong reservations, is an example to us all.

In my opinion, Ananias's acceptance of Saul was absolutely
crucial in his development into the person we know as Paul the
apostle. The question is, how ready are we to accept people fully
into fellowship? Who knows how God may be going to use
some of them in the future? My prayer is that God will make

the Church a community where all transformed outcasts are welcomed and accepted.

The challenge of action

Throughout His ministry, Jesus continually reached out to those who were considered to be outcasts from society. Down the years, the Christian Church has successfully sought in many ways to follow the Master's example in reaching out to the poor, needy, diseased, neglected, marginalized and disadvantaged of the world.

The challenge for the Church today is to continue to be at the cutting edge of such action, showing God's love and mercy in practical ways, always being prepared to reach out and touch those regarded as untouchable.

CHAPTER SEVEN

WHO NEEDS PHYSIOTHERAPY?

[Jesus heals a paralysed man]

Mark 2:1-12
(also Matthew 9:2-8; Luke 5:18-26)

Introduction

It is significant that *Mark* places this miracle immediately after the one where the man is healed of leprosy. In chapter 6 we saw how leprosy was and still is a commonly used symbol for sin; in this chapter we look at the only miracle connected with the forgiveness of sins.

What are friends for?

Isn't it good to have friends who care? And these friends not only care, but are so moved with compassion that four of them pick up their paralysed friend as he lies there helplessly on his mat, and bring him to Jesus. Their task would have been rather more awkward if beds then had been as they are now; but in those days mats were the norm, so it was fairly straightforward for them.

Like hundreds of others, the friends have heard how Jesus has been healing the sick, and this has inspired their faith to the point where all of them believe that Jesus can and will heal their friend. And together they put their faith into action *(3)*.

What a challenge this is to us to be an inspiration and encouragement to those around us who are in need, not only physically but also spiritually and emotionally. So often we think that having faith is the responsibility of the individual. While that is obviously very important, we need to have faith on behalf of others, too, and to get alongside them, supporting their faith.

In my experience, corporate faith is very powerful. There is something exciting and inspirational about a group of people coming together in faith to pray about a person or an issue, joining their faith together as they bring the individual or situation before God.

The faith level of the group often has a marked effect on the faith level of the individual. The uncomfortable question that we need to address in our churches is this: when we come together, do we speak words of expectant, believing faith, or is the prevailing ethos purely one of sympathy for and acceptance of the situation? I believe that it is vitally important that we realize our collective responsibility, and are instrumental as a group in bringing people in faith to Jesus.

There's a hole in my roof . . .

So the men find out where Jesus is in town, and make their way there, only to find *'So many gathered that there was no room left, not even outside the door' (2)*.

Isn't it amazing how many obstacles occur when we try to bring people to Jesus? I can imagine the groans that went round the group of friends as they came round the corner and saw all the people gathered outside the house. Some of them were probably of the opinion that they might as well turn round and take their paralysed friend back home straight away, on the grounds that they could always try again another time. And then one of them had a bright idea.

In those days, houses were built of stone. They had flat roofs which were usually made up of a thick layer of mud or clay mixed with straw, packed with a stone roller, and supported by mats of branches across wooden beams. There was a stairway outside which led on to the roof. So for the four friends it was simply a matter of carrying the paralysed man up the stairs and onto the roof. I wonder what he had to say about all this.

Once that had been achieved, the rest was relatively easy. *Mark* tells us: *'they made an opening in the roof above Jesus and, after digging through it, lowered the mat the paralysed man was lying on'* *(4)*. This just shows how determined they were to get their paralysed friend to Jesus.

It's quite a comical scene really. There's Jesus in full flow, as He *'preached the word to them' (2)*, when suddenly lumps of mud, bits of straw and chips of wood start dropping down on Him. I imagine the people who are listening not only being distracted by this, but wondering whether to laugh or pretend it isn't happening. The way I see it, Jesus stops talking, looks up, and then, with a broad smile on His face, moves out of the way as the mud, straw and wood continue to rain down from above. I don't suppose the owner of the house was best pleased about what was happening though. Whatever was he going to write on his house insurance claim form?

Eventually the hole is big enough for the paralysed man still lying on his mat to be lowered through, presumably by means of ropes, which one of the friends has had to go and get, and down to where Jesus is.

Pardon?

Mark's account continues: *'When Jesus saw their faith' (5a)*. No words of faith are expressed here, either from the friends above or the paralysed man below. Nobody says anything. It is the *action* they have taken and the lengths to which they have gone which speak out their corporate faith far more eloquently than words could ever have done. And Jesus always responds to faith.

But His response isn't at all what the paralysed man is expecting. *Mark* tells us that Jesus *'said to the paralytic, "Son, your sins are forgiven"'* (5b). At which point I imagine the man thinking: 'Pardon? That's not what I was expecting to hear. "Be healed" was more what I was hoping for.'

There are often times when we come to God in faith, and His response is nothing like what we are expecting. And that is because God is sovereign and supernatural. He deals with us according to His own sovereign ways, time and will; and with His supernatural knowledge He knows exactly what the root of the problem is, what the real need is, and what must be tackled first. It is true to say that, in every case, our deepest need is for God's forgiveness.

Jesus is emphasizing both to the paralysed man and to the crowd that having their sins forgiven is more important than being physically healed. At which point the man must have thought: 'Pardon? Can all my sins really be pardoned? Can I really be forgiven for all the wrong things I've done?'

Sickness and sin

Jesus is making full use here of the Jewish belief that sickness was sometimes caused by sin. One contemporary Jewish rabbi is reported to have said that 'there is no sick man healed of his sickness until all his sins have been forgiven him.'

It is more than likely that the paralysed man believed this, thinking that he was ill because God was punishing him. Jesus would have known this, and therefore He tackles this fundamental issue first. Once again, we see Jesus' concern for the whole person.

What joy Jesus' words must have caused to rise within the man. God was not angry with him; he was not living under God's judgement; he was being accepted into the family of God. Jesus even called him *'Son'* (5). This is a further indication to everyone that none of us is rejected by God on account of his sin; God's forgiveness extends to each one of us, and we are all welcome in His family, where He is our loving Father.

Blatant blasphemy

Mark doesn't tell us what the reaction of the crowd was to these words of Jesus. My guess is either stunned silence or gasps of amazement, followed by low whispers as the news rippled out to the crowds in the street outside. Even the teachers of the Law were silent, though their minds were working overtime. *'"Why does this fellow talk like that? He's blaspheming! Who can forgive sins but God alone?"' (7).*

According to the theology of the Jews, even the Messiah could not forgive sins. So by claiming to be able to do this, Jesus was, in fact, stating that He was greater even than the promised Messiah; He was actually claiming to be God Himself. Under Jewish Law, anyone claiming to be God, or having majesty and authority belonging only to God, was guilty of blasphemy, the punishment for which was death by stoning *(Leviticus 24:16)*. It was this charge of which Jesus would be found guilty by the Sanhedrin, the Jewish Council *(Mark 14:61-64)*, and it would lead eventually to His crucifixion by the Romans.

For the time being, though, they kept their thoughts to themselves. Or so they believed. But Jesus knew exactly what they were thinking *(8)*, and His purpose was to show them that what He had said to the paralysed man was undeniably true, and was not blasphemy at all.

A question of proof

And Jesus does it by first of all asking them a question: *'"Which is easier: to say to the paralytic, 'Your sins are forgiven,' or to say, 'Get up, take your mat and walk'?"' (9)* I imagine Jesus pausing at this point to let the significance of His question sink in. It could be said that both statements are just as easy to say; so what point is Jesus making? It's all about proof.

Can it be proved that a person's sins have been forgiven? Obviously not: it's a matter of faith. I believe by faith and on the authority of God's Word (for example *1 John 1:9*) that I have been forgiven and cleansed from my sin, and I have an assurance about that in my mind and in my spirit.

Can it be proved that a paralysed man has been healed? It certainly can: it's a matter of sight. We can all see the cure for ourselves, and it can be verified by the medical profession. So in that sense it is easier to say *'Get up and walk'*, because that can be seen to have happened and be conclusively verified. That is why Jesus links the two conditions together by saying: *' "But that you may know that the Son of Man has authority on earth to forgive sins" . . . . He said to the paralytic, "I tell you, get up, take your mat and go home" '* (10, 11).

The fact that the paralytic is healed, which can be seen, shows that he has also been forgiven, which can't be seen. It is a visible sign of an invisible truth. The proof of the forgiving is in the healing. Jesus is stating quite categorically that just as He can heal, so He can forgive. And this means that any charge of blasphemy is completely unfounded.

Son of Man

The title 'Son of Man' is the one that Jesus uses most frequently to describe Himself: in fact, it appears eighty-one times in the gospels. In *Mark* he uses it fourteen times: twice as often as the title 'Messiah', which means the same as 'Christ'. There is still much discussion about what this title actually means, although it is clearly something to do with the fact that Jesus was fully human as well as fully divine ['Son of God'].

Many years before, the prophet Daniel *(7:13, 14)* had a vision of the coming of a heavenly figure who would set up an ever-lasting kingdom. He called him 'son of man'. Jesus, throughout His ministry, certainly seems to have identified Himself as this person, culminating in His statement during His trial before the Jewish Council *(Mark 14:62)*.

Crisis of faith

Meanwhile, back on the mat, the paralysed man is suddenly aware that Jesus has turned His attention away from the teachers of the Law and back to him. Has he heard what Jesus has said correctly? Did He really say 'Get up'?

Up to now, it has been this man's friends who have been putting their faith into action. Now it's his turn. How is he going to respond to Jesus' command? This is a crisis point for him: a crisis of faith.

The paralytic could have just lain there on his mat, looking up at Jesus, thinking to himself, quite reasonably: 'Get up? I've never been able to get up in my life. I've seen others do it, but I'm not sure I know how to do it. Besides which, I can't get up: I'm paralysed. I've always been paralysed. How can I possibly get up? And even if I do try to get up, I'll probably just fall flat on my face, and all these people will laugh at me. I'll be the butt of jokes for years to come. On the whole, I think I'll just stay where I am after all.' And the chance for healing would have passed him by. The opportunity to have his life transformed would have gone, probably for ever.

But the man didn't. He responded by putting his faith into practice. He obeyed Jesus, even though he probably still had doubts and fears in his mind; even though it took all the courage he could muster to begin to move those atrophied limbs. What a wonderful experience he must have had of the power of God surging through his paralysed body as he began to move in response to Jesus' command. And the more he moved, the more he found he could move, until he was on his feet in front of them all. *Mark* simply says: *'He got up.' (12a)*. But, as we have seen, it wasn't quite as simple as that.

Many years ago, I broke my leg playing football. When I was finally out of plaster, I had to attend physiotherapy regularly at the hospital to assist me to walk and bend the knee properly again. It took several weeks of exercise, which was painful at times, to restore my leg to anything like full working order.

This man required no physiotherapy whatsoever. So triumphantly had he come through his crisis of faith that he could not only get up, but he could stand, bend fully down to his mat lying there on the ground, use his arms to roll it up, and walk unaided all the way home *(12a)*. He was completely cured, with all his muscles, joints, bones, sinews and tendons working perfectly and painlessly. No wonder *'This amazed everyone'* and resulted in spontaneous praise *(12b)*.

Trust and obey

There are times in our lives when we, too, come to a crisis of faith: a point where God speaks to us quite clearly and requires us to take a step of faith. Or it may be that a situation arises over which we have no control, and God tells us to have faith in Him, because this did not take Him by surprise, and He is in control.

The question is, how do we respond at the crisis point? Let's take our example from this paralysed man. He did not allow his perfectly reasonable doubts, his lack of understanding about how his healing was going to be possible, his fear of other people and what they might say, or any other negatives that might have gone through his mind to stop him from responding to Jesus. He was prepared to trust and obey.

Spiritual paralysis

It is quite possible for us to be perfectly healthy physically, and yet to be paralysed spiritually. This means that God can't use us until we are prepared to allow Him to deal with whatever are the causes of our paralysis.

Our attitudes to others are a common cause of spiritual paralysis. We may feel bitter, resentful or unforgiving towards someone. We may hold grievances against people, or be judgemental about what others have done. Other common causes include: habits that we know are wrong but we hang on to; a self-consciousness that is more concerned with what other people may think and say rather than with what God thinks and says; events from our past which come back to haunt us; the circumstances that we are in at the moment.

God does not want us to be paralysed by any of these things, or by anything else for that matter. Yet in a sense He is powerless to deal with our paralysis until we come to Him. Sometimes it can be so difficult and painful that we need the support and help of friends to bring us to God in the first place.

But when we come into God's presence and humble ourselves before Him, we know that we are going to hear those wonderful words 'Get up!' For there is no form of paralysis binding us from which the power of God cannot free us, provided we want to be free from it. God may require us to take certain courses of action, and these may not be easy, but are an essential part of our rehabilitation process. Unlike the paralysed man, we may require physiotherapy to restore us to being people who, in every sense of the word, are fit for the Master's use.

CHAPTER EIGHT

A TOUCHING ENCOUNTER

[Jesus heals a sick woman]
Mark 5:22-34
(also Matthew 9:20-22; Luke 8:42-48)

Introduction

This miracle takes place in Capernaum as Jesus is on His way to the house of a man named Jairus, whose daughter is dying [see chapter 18].

At the time of Jesus, women were very much regarded as second-class citizens, an attitude enshrined in Jewish Law. The fact that Jesus is on His way to heal a young woman when He is involved in the healing of another woman is a double indication of Jesus' different attitude to women. He treats them as being of equal value and importance with men: a radical and ground-breaking approach for a teacher of His day, and for centuries to come.

Alone and afflicted

Mark tells us that *'A large crowd followed and pressed around him' (24)*. And in that large throng of people jostling around Jesus is a woman in desperate need. For the past twelve years she has been *'subject to bleeding' (25)*. The exact nature of her condition is not known. It might have been a menstrual problem that had become a constant haemorrhage, leaving her weak and exhausted. According to the Jewish Law, this would make her ritually unclean: an outcast; an untouchable, rather like the man with leprosy. This meant that she was not allowed to worship as one of God's chosen people *(Leviticus 15:25-33)*.

And if that wasn't enough to put up with, the woman would also have been shunned by the community, because those touching her would have made themselves unclean *(15:27)*. Her existence would therefore have been one of miserable isolation.

The fact that people in the crowd seem not to bother about brushing against the woman as they move along seems to suggest either that she doesn't live in Capernaum, or that the people are far too preoccupied with what Jesus is doing to notice her.

From riches to rags

Mark tells us that *'She had suffered a great deal under the care of many doctors and had spent all she had, yet instead of getting better she grew worse' (26)*. It is interesting, though perhaps not surprising, to notice that Luke, a doctor himself, is a little less frank about the shortcomings of his medical colleagues in his account of this incident *(8:43)*.

In those days, it was a matter of paying for each consultation, and this had eaten into the woman's finances. The Jewish Talmud, which was like a handbook to the Torah or Law of Moses, actually contains a record of the medicines and treatments prescribed for illnesses.

The sick lady must have been quite well off to start with, because she has been consulting various doctors over a period of twelve years. But now she finds herself destitute. This must have been particularly difficult for her to come to terms with, if we bear in mind her likely background and status in society. She may even have been thrown out by her family. This woman of independent means is now reduced to being dependent on the means and charity of others. There is no benefits system in place to come to her aid. She has become the sort of person she used to despise. What a bitter pill for her to have to swallow: far more difficult than the ones the doctors give her.

Resourceless but resourceful

The woman had reached the end of her resources. Sometimes we can rely too much on our own resources, and not enough on God's. Whereas our resources are finite, His are infinite. I know that I am often guilty of trying to resolve situations in my own strength, only to find that I am actually making matters worse. But when I run out of ideas, I know that God has the perfect solution, and I wonder why I didn't turn to Him sooner.

Then the woman hears about Jesus *(27a)*, and a bold thought forms in her mind *(28)*. It's a thought that is full of faith: she is in no doubt that healing will be hers. She has probably heard that Jesus has touched many people as they have come to Him for healing. But she doesn't want to approach Him in that way, maybe because she is afraid that some people in the crowd will recognize her if she draws attention to herself publicly.

Fear can so often prevent us from approaching God. Fear that God might be angry with us for what we have done or not done; fear of what might happen, or of what might be required of us; fear of what other people might think of us, or say about us; all kinds of fears.

It is right and proper that we fear God in the sense that we hold Him in awe, for He is the Almighty, the Omniscient Creator and Sustainer of all things. But He is also our Father and we are His children, whom He has loved with an everlasting love. It is His desire that we come into His presence to confess our sins, to worship Him and to present our petitions to Him. We must never let fear hold us back from approaching Him.

Perhaps the woman thinks Jesus may not have time for her as He is hurrying to get to Jairus' house. It is wonderful to realize that God is never too busy to listen to us, even though we are often too busy to listen to God. He never takes the phone off the hook: He has always got time for us.

It could be that the woman doesn't want to ask Jesus to make Himself unclean by touching her, even though she may have known that He has touched a leper. Sometimes we feel that the very nature of our problem keeps us from God. How wonderful it is to know that God is always ready and willing to help, no matter what our misgivings.

Whatever the reason, the woman is convinced that if healing comes to those whom Jesus touches, it should happen to those who touch Jesus. I imagine her purposefully excusing her way through the crowd to get to the front, at the same time working her way round so that she is directly behind Jesus. Perhaps not quite to the front: just close enough to enable her to stretch out her arm through the front row to touch Jesus' cloak (27), and then melt away into the distance.

A ridiculous question

The effect is immediate. The symptoms disappear, and the woman is convinced that the cause has been dealt with too (29). This miracle is unique because the woman is cured without Jesus' knowing about her being there. But Jesus does know that someone has touched His cloak in faith, because He feels power go out of Him (30a). The supernatural power of God within Jesus responds to the touch of faith.

As soon as Jesus realizes what has happened, He does something very significant. *Mark* tells us that *'He turned around in the crowd' (30b)*. He knows that He has been touched in faith from behind rather than from the side, or for that matter from the front, as the crowd are apparently all around Him.

Looking at that section of the throng, Jesus then asks what appears to everyone else to be a rather ridiculous question: *'"Who touched my clothes?"' (30c)*. The disciples voice what the crowd must all be thinking (31). There are so many people jostling around and brushing up against Jesus that hundreds must have touched Him.

To their surprise, Jesus persists. *Luke* tells us: *'But Jesus said, "Someone touched me; I know that power has gone out from me"' (8:46)*. *Mark* says: *'Jesus kept looking around to see who had done it' (32)*. Jesus is determined that there will be no misunderstanding here. He wants to make it quite clear that He is not wearing some kind of magic cloak, as some of the wonder-workers of the day claimed to do. It is the faith of the woman that has brought about her cure, not the fact that she has touched His clothes. That action has merely been a means of expressing her faith. Once again we are reminded that faith without actions isn't faith at all *(James 2:17)*.

Confession of faith

By this time, the woman realizes that she has no alternative but to confess, and does so in fear and trembling *(33)*. To her surprise, Jesus does not speak words of anger, but words of peace. He calls her 'Daughter' *(34)*, in the same way that He called the paralysed man 'Son' *(2:5b)*, to reassure her that she is part of God's family. He confirms to her that she has been fully cured of her problem, at the same time making it clear both to the woman herself and to the whole crowd that it is her faith alone that has caused her to be healed *(34a)*.

It is comforting and reassuring to know that when we come to Jesus we shall not be greeted with words of anger, condemnation and judgement, but rather with words of peace, love and forgiveness.

CHAPTER NINE

BLIND MAN'S FAITH

[Blind Bartimaeus receives his sight]
Mark 10:46-52
(also Luke 18:35-43)

Introduction

This is the last miracle of healing recorded by *Mark*. It happened towards the end of Jesus' ministry as He was on His way to Jerusalem to declare Himself openly as the Messiah. This would precipitate the events leading to His arrest, trial, crucifixion and resurrection.

Jericho

Jesus has spent most of His time in the northern district of Galilee. He is now making His way to Jerusalem, which is situated in the south of the country of Palestine in the region of Judaea. His journey there takes Him through Jericho *(46a)*, a very ancient city located some fifteen miles to the north east of Jerusalem.

The old city of Jericho, whose walls had miraculously collapsed before Joshua and his army *(see Joshua 6)*, had mostly been abandoned. A new city had been built by Herod the Great to the south of the old one. Herod was the king of Judaea at the time when Jesus was born *(Matthew 2:1)*.

It beggars belief

Beggars were a common sight along the roads near the cities.

They were usually people with some kind of physical disability which prevented them from earning a living. There wasn't the medical help then that exists now to support them. Nor was there any financial assistance. Not only were there no disability benefits; there was little response from the people to their obligation to provide for the needy under the Law of Moses *(Leviticus 25:35-38)*. The Care in the Community principle enshrined in the Law was largely ignored. Responsibility to others was as unpopular then as it often is now. And the result was beggars everywhere: people without hope in the world.

In this sense, we were all once beggars: without hope until we met Jesus. And we are surrounded by many people in a similar situation, who also need to meet Jesus. Like Bartimaeus, not only were we beggars but we were also blind and in need of having our eyes opened: not physically, but spiritually. A person blind from birth has a physical dimension missing from his life and existence. In the same way, all of us are blind to the spiritual dimension of life, until we come to Jesus and ask Him to open our eyes. And suddenly we see things as they really are, in their true perspective, illuminated by the light of God.

John Newton, once the captain of a slave ship, had his eyes opened by Jesus. To try to express how he felt, he wrote the words of the song 'Amazing Grace', in which he included this line: 'I once was blind, but now I see.'

Passing by

Imagine this poor, blind beggar, probably dressed in little more than rags, sitting by the side of the road leading from Jericho to Jerusalem, along with scores of other beggars with varying disabilities, all against the backdrop of the magnificent city walls. Today he has shuffled his way, as he does every day, to this particular spot, from where he makes his pitch to the passersby, many of whom are pilgrims making their way to Jerusalem, the Holy City.

But today is going to be different: a day the beggar will never forget. With his acute sense of hearing he is aware of a noise in the distance. It's not the usual chatter of the twos or threes or even small groups of people who usually pass him by, although some do stop and offer him a crust or throw him a coin. No: it's definitely a crowd of people, and a large crowd at that, who are getting ever closer to where he is sitting.

What's going on? What's happening? This is not the usual sound of a crowd. There's something different about it. A sense of excitement in the air. Hard to explain, but definitely there.

Unable to contain himself any longer, the blind man shouts his questions to anyone who will listen. Eventually, a reply comes his way. ' "Jesus of Nazareth is passing by" ' (Luke 18:37). Jesus of Nazareth? *The* Jesus of Nazareth? The one who heals the sick, makes the lame walk and the blind see? No wonder Bartimaeus begins to shout, ' "Jesus, Son of David, have mercy on me!" ' (Mark 10:47).

Here we see this important principle once again. Jesus graciously comes where we are, but, as we saw in chapter 5, He will pass by unless we cry out to Him. He comes by invitation only.

Son of David

This is the only place in the whole of *Mark* where this title is used. Jews believed that when the Messiah came He would be a descendant of the greatest king in their history: King David. So 'Son of David' became a popular title for the Messiah. However, to voice a title such as this in public risked drawing the attention of the Romans, not only to the person doing the shouting but also to the person to whom it was addressed.

Until now, Jesus has made every effort to keep the fact that He is the Messiah secret [see chapter 6]. But on this occasion He neither rebukes Bartimaeus for having used the title, nor does He tell him to keep quiet about what has been done for him. The time for secrecy is over. Matters are about to come to a head in Jerusalem.

It is interesting that Bartimaeus cries to the 'Son of David' for mercy, rather than specifically for sight. Perhaps he thinks that a more general cry for help is more likely to be heeded than a specific request for a personal miracle.

The voices of the crowd

The reaction of many of the people in the crowd is predictable: *'Many rebuked him and told him to be quiet' (48a)*. Perhaps some of them were genuinely concerned about his using the Messianic title, and the consequences that might have for Jesus. However, it seems more likely that they were letting their prejudices show. It was as if they were saying: 'You're an outcast, a beggar, an inferior, a nobody. Jesus is far too busy to have time for a down-and-out like you. So just be quiet; accept your lot, and get on with it without making all this fuss.'

The epistle of *James* is very strong indeed on the subject of prejudice in the church, showing in no uncertain terms that to discriminate between people or to practise favouritism is wrong *(2:1-13)*. Yet it is so easy to fall into this trap and to find ourselves adopting incorrect attitudes, just as many in this crowd were guilty of doing.

Those voices were out to stop the man's voice being heard. He was being crowded out. And there are many voices that would seek to stop us calling out to Jesus. Voices that say things like: 'What will people say?' 'You don't know what you're doing.' 'You're just getting all emotional.' 'What about all the things you don't understand?' 'That's all right for those religious types, but not for you.' And many other things besides. Bartimaeus shows us how to respond on such occasions.

It's so very easy to find ourselves listening to the wrong voices. It's a good idea to ask ourselves frequently which voices we are listening to, and why.

Resist and persist

So what was Bartimaeus's response to being treated like that? Did he retreat into his shell, cowed by the crowd? Not a bit of it! *Mark* tells us, *'but he shouted all the more, "Son of David, have mercy on me!"' (48b)*.

You've got to admire the man. The rebukes he has received are enough to put most people off: but they just make Bartimaeus even more determined. He refuses to be pressurized by those around him, and persists in crying out for mercy. He doesn't care what other people think about him and his situation. This is an opportunity that may never come his way again. He realizes the significance of the moment, and seizes it with both hands. The Messiah is passing by, and he has the simple faith to believe that the 'Son of David' can do something for him. And his persistence has its reward.

Like Bartimaeus, may we too have the courage to resist and to persist: to resist being pressurized by those around us who would seek to keep us from God, whose voices are constantly there; and to persist in calling out to God in prayer.

Jesus told not one but two parables to show us how important it is to be persistent in our prayers, and not to be put off or give up *(see Luke 11:5-8; 18:1-8)*. It is so much easier to stop praying, particularly when nothing seems to be happening. That is when our faith in God is really put to the test. But be encouraged: Jesus teaches us through those parables that persistent prayer will be rewarded.

Stop . . .

'Jesus stopped' (49a). What significant words these are. Here is Jesus, with His mind set on what lies ahead of Him in Jerusalem, surrounded by a noisy crowd. Yet He hears the persistent cries of a blind beggar, and has time for him: time to stop and meet with him face to face. It would be easy for the shouts of Bartimaeus to be lost in the general noise of the crowd. It would be understandable for Jesus, with all that is on His mind, to ignore the beggar's pleas. But He doesn't. He responds to the faith which underpins the blind man's desperate cries. He draws near to where he is; then He stops and says, *'"Call him"'* *(49a)*.

Jesus doesn't actually go to Bartimaeus: He expects Bartimaeus to come to Him. And Bartimaeus responds with alacrity to the call of Jesus as communicated to him by people in the crowd *(49b, 50)*. No half-hearted response here: just wholehearted, energetic, even frenzied action. He throws; he jumps; he comes. Away goes the cloak with which he covers himself, and which restricts his movement. Up he jumps as fast as he can, not taking the usual care that he would have taken. And he can't come to Jesus quickly enough. Suddenly, he's there, standing in front of the One in whom he has placed his hope.

Another ridiculous question

And then he hears Jesus asking him what he probably thinks is a rather ridiculous question. *'"What do you want me to do for you?"' (51a)*. Surely it is obvious? Does he really have to spell it out? Apparently so. *'"Rabbi, I want to see"' (51b)*.

There are two important points here. Firstly, Jesus requires him to be specific. The blind beggar has many needs. Which one does he want Jesus to address? Where specifically does he want God's *'mercy' (47, 48)* to be shown? When we come to God in prayer, he wants us to be specific rather than make general requests. Specific prayers can be seen to have been answered, with the result that due praise can be given to God, as it was in the case of this healing *(Luke 18:43)*.

Secondly, it is essential that Bartimaeus hands the problem over to Jesus of his own free will, and submits it to Him to deal with. Here again we see the importance of this principle. Jesus never healed anyone against their will, and God never intervenes in any of our problems unless we hand them over to Him.

Go . . .

Once again we see how faith is required for healing to take place, and the immediacy of Jesus' response to it. *'"Go," said Jesus, "your faith has healed you." Immediately he received his sight' (52)*, and he could see Jesus face to face. Because Jesus stopped, Bartimaeus could go *(49, 52)*.

Never having been blind, I can only imagine how wonderful

it must be to have one's sight restored and suddenly to be aware of a whole new dimension to life which changes everything. What would Bartimaeus do with his transformed life? Where would he 'go'? He could have gone back to Jericho, with his life changed, thanks to his meeting with Jesus, yet not really going anywhere as a result. But he made a different choice. Instead, he *'followed Jesus along the road' (52b)*.

Being a disciple is all about following Jesus on the road. New experiences in God and learning more about Him are just two of the rich rewards which lie in store for us as we go with God.

The road of discipleship

The road from Jericho to Jerusalem was a difficult, even a dangerous one. Jesus had already used it as the setting for the parable of the Good Samaritan *(Luke 10:25-37)*, except that the traveller who was attacked was actually going in the opposite direction.

Jesus never said that following Him would be easy. He said that anyone wishing to be His disciple must *'"deny himself, take up his cross and follow me"' (Mark 8:34)*. On another occasion, He told His disciples: *'In this world you will have trouble' (John 16:33)*. There will be many ups and downs, trials and joys along the road of pilgrimage that leads from Jericho, our worldly home which we leave behind as we begin our walk with God, to our glorious destination, the new Jerusalem, the City of God, our heavenly home *(Revelation 21)*.

CHAPTER TEN

THE BLIND INVESTIGATE THE BLIND

[Jesus heals a man born blind]

John 9:1-41

Introduction

This is another occasion when Jesus restores the sight of a blind man, and it provides some interesting contrasts with the healing of Bartimaeus.

'Who sinned?'

The Jews believed that blindness was a curse from God for sin, hence the disciples' question *(2)*. In fact, the Jews considered that any suffering or calamity was the consequence of sin. As the rabbis of the day put it: 'There is no suffering without iniquity.'

The sin itself need not have been committed by the person who was afflicted. As in the case of a child born blind, this was seen as being the result of parental sin, although some rabbis even believed that children could actually sin in the womb.

Jesus makes it quite clear that such beliefs are completely misguided, and the fact that He intends to heal this man is further proof that his affliction is in no way a punishment from God, nor is it the consequence of sin *(3)*.

The wrong question

Living in a fallen world means that innocent people are going to suffer. Whatever the reason for our suffering might be, Jesus has the power to help us to deal with it, and will give us the strength to cope with it.

When we suffer, we frequently ask the wrong question. Our response is often 'Why?' as in 'Why me? Why is this happening to me? Why am I in this situation?' The question we should really be asking is 'What?' For example, 'What can I learn from this situation? What is it teaching me about God and about myself? What new experiences of God is this bringing into my life? What can I learn from all this that I can use to help others?' I accept that only an exceptional person can put the 'What' question if he is suffering from the crippling pain of arthritis or enduring daily doses of chemotherapy, but I know of many instances in which God has entered – upon invitation – the darkest of pictures, and transformed them.

Here's mud for your eyes

How about this for an unusual method of treatment? *'He spit on the ground, made some mud with the saliva, and put it on the man's eyes' (6)*. Jesus usually cured by touch or by word: by mud is not only unexpected but is unique in the gospels. I wonder what His disciples, not to mention the bystanders, thought as they saw Jesus engaged in making this extraordinary preparation.

True, the disciples had seen Jesus use saliva before to bring sight to a blind man in Bethsaida *(Mark 8:22-25)*. On that occasion, the man had been healed in two stages, which is the only recorded miracle where that happened. This shows that healing can be gradual as well as instantaneous.

That blind man had been brought to Jesus for healing. Blind Bartimaeus had persistently called out to Jesus for mercy, as we saw in chapter 9. But this blind man has neither been brought to Jesus, nor has he asked for healing. Faith has not been expressed by him or on his behalf. And this is the key to understanding this rather bizarre action of Jesus.

Sent to 'Sent'

Having put the mud preparation on the eyes of the blind man, who must have wondered what on earth was going on, Jesus tells him to '"*Go, . . . wash in the Pool of Siloam*"' (7a). The Pool of Siloam had been built by King Hezekiah (715-686 BC) to allow the inhabitants of Jerusalem access to water within the city walls. This was particularly important in times of siege.

John tells us that the word 'Siloam' means 'Sent', and it can also be translated 'one who has been sent'. Which is exactly what the blind man was. The question is, did he go? By His actions, Jesus had created an opportunity for the man to show his faith. He was given the choice. Either he could stand there, wipe the mud away from his eyes, and carry on as if nothing had happened; or he could show his faith by being obedient to Jesus' command, going to the pool and washing as instructed, believing that his sight would be restored if he did.

John tells us what his decision was: *'So the man went and washed, and came home seeing'* (7b). There is no suggestion that anyone else went with him: he had to have the courage of his own convictions and go alone. Which serves to emphasize the point that faith is something we have to put into practice for ourselves: no one else can do it for us. Others can encourage us and pray for us, but ultimately we have to take the step alone. And how wonderfully the man's faith was vindicated.

The Pharisees

On seeing that the blind man's sight has been restored, some of his neighbours are incredulous, while others are dubious (8, 9b). On hearing the man's insistence that it really is he (9c), they demand an explanation (10). This he duly gives (11), but it doesn't seem to satisfy them; so they take him to the Pharisees (13).

The Pharisees were in charge of the synagogues, so they wielded a great deal of power in the community. There was a synagogue in nearly every town or village. The people used to go there every Sabbath day to hear the Scriptures read and explained by the Pharisees, to worship and to pray. They were not priests, but they were very well-educated people who enjoyed nothing better than debates about the Jewish Law, which they prided themselves on following to the letter. Not only did they obey the Torah, which had been given to Moses by God, and was therefore also called the Law of Moses; they obeyed the Mishna as well.

The Mishna is a collection of teachings given by rabbis down the years in their attempts to explain the Torah and make it clearer for the people to understand and put into practice. For example, the Torah said that a person was not to work on the Sabbath day, but it didn't define the word 'work'. The Mishna lists everything that the rabbis classed as 'work', so that the people would know what was forbidden on the Sabbath. It also laid down all kinds of rules, covering everything from the ceremonial, such as washing, right through to correct behaviour in all parts of daily family life. In other words, it was like a man-made handbook to the God-given Torah. The Pharisees considered the Mishna to be just as important as the Torah, and this brought them into sharp conflict with Jesus, who condemned them as hypocrites, and used several other choice phrases to describe them *(Matthew 23:1-36)*.

The Pharisees opposed Jesus all the way along the line. This was basically because they were jealous of Him: jealous of His popularity with the people, which they could not achieve; jealous of the miracles He performed, which they could not do; jealous of the fact that He taught with an authority which they could not match. Of all the people in Palestine, they should have been the ones to recognize Jesus as the promised Messiah; but they steadfastly refused to acknowledge Him as such, preferring to maintain their position and their power. Instead of pointing the people to Jesus the Messiah, they made every effort to turn the people against Him. It was before such men that the man born blind was brought.

The miracle investigated

This section contains some lovely moments provided by the simplicity of the healed man's reasoning juxtaposed with the complexity of that of the Pharisees.

- #### Divisive dilemma

First of all, the Pharisees seek to ascertain the facts of what happened, which the man gives them most succinctly: *'"He put mud on my eyes . . . and I washed, and now I see"'* (15). This causes division among them straight away *(16)*. Jesus has healed the man on the Sabbath, an act which the Mishna classes as 'work', not to mention the work involved in the making of the mud application, and is therefore forbidden. This makes Jesus a law breaker, a sinner. As far as many of them are concerned, this clearly shows therefore that Jesus cannot possibly be *'from God'* *(16a)*. Others of them reasoned that if Jesus was in fact a sinner, then how could He *'do such miraculous signs?'* *(16b)*. This group among them realize that the power to enable Jesus to do this miracle can have come only from God. A dilemma indeed.

- #### Discredit Jesus

Having debated for some time and been unable to resolve this dilemma, the Pharisees now try a different tack. They question the man about Jesus in what seems to me to be a rather sarcastic manner: *'"What have you to say about him? It was your eyes he opened"'(17b)*.

Far from being overawed by the situation, the man seems to be gaining in confidence and boldness. His faith in Jesus and his belief about who Jesus is just keeps on growing. He had described Jesus as a 'man' when questioned by his neighbours *(11)*. In reply to the Pharisees, he is now convinced that *'"He is a prophet"'* *(17c)*. Hardly the reply they were hoping for.

- #### Discredit the witness

The Pharisees, probably taken aback by the man's forthrightness, and not wanting to be further divided over whether

Jesus is a prophet or not, change tack yet again. Having failed to discredit Jesus, they decide to try to discredit the witness to Jesus by casting doubt on whether he was actually blind in the first place *(18)*. Which just goes to show that if people don't want to believe, they'll find reasons not to, however *un*reasonable these might be.

The Pharisees send for the man's parents, who must have been dreading this moment. They are in a difficult position, torn between loyalty to and support for their son, and fear of being thrown out of the synagogue if their answers do not please the Pharisees. This is a very real threat, which could mean their being cut off from all social relationships and ostracized by the whole community.

The parents manage to negotiate the situation quite cleverly. They are loyal to their son by confirming his blindness from birth *(20)*, but they put the responsibility for what has happened firmly in his court *(21)*. This includes what opinion he may have formed about Jesus: that's down to him, and is nothing to do with us; *'"He is of age; ask him"' (21b-23)*.

• *Solid ground*

The Pharisees do ask him, but this time with an explicit command to tell the truth: *'"Give glory to God"' (24b)*. This is almost the identical sentence used by Joshua when confronting a man called Achan about his sin *(Joshua 7:19, 20)*. The Pharisees further pressurize the man by going on to say: *'"We know this man [Jesus] is a sinner"' (24c)*. And the word used for 'we' in Greek, the language in which the New Testament was originally written, is emphatic, so the implication is clear. What they are really saying is: *We* know he's a sinner, and *you* had better agree with us.

The man's response is to speak the truth as requested, simply and boldly, but without being influenced by the implication behind the Pharisees' statement. *'"Whether he is a sinner or not, I don't know. One thing I do know. I was blind but now I see!"' (25)*. This is the one irrefutable truth that cannot be denied. And it is to this fact that the man keeps going back *(11, 15, 25, 30)*. This is the solid ground of experience on which he stands. He can't match the intellectual gymnastics of the Pharisees, even if he wants to. But he knows what has happened to him: an experience which no one can deny or disprove.

There are times when we may feel unable to explain the finer points of our faith in a deep theological way. Times when we may find it difficult to win an intellectual argument about our beliefs. This happened to me in my university days when following a Religious Studies course. Having left the shelter of my church and home for the first time, I found myself surrounded by lecturers presenting arguments, which I had never met before, that challenged my faith and beliefs, and which I found difficult to counter. This was a very unsettling experience, and at times the only ground I had to stand on which could not be denied or disproved was the solid ground of my experience of Jesus Christ as my Lord and Saviour, and the transformation of my life and attitudes as a result of my encounter with Him.

Even though I like to think that I can now confidently enter into such intellectual debates, the fact remains that, in my experience, a far more effective weapon is the statement of a simple personal faith in Jesus Christ. That is the rock on which we stand. That is the rock on which Jesus told Peter He was going to build His Church *(Matthew 16:15-18)*. The rock of our faith in Jesus Christ, the Son of God, our Saviour, as expressed by the Early Church in the symbol of the fish [see chapter 4].

So there is no need for us to feel daunted when we find ourselves in similar situations to the one faced by the man born blind. He stuck to his guns, and simply but boldly shared his testimony. May God give us the courage to do the same.

• *Simply logical*

However, the Pharisees will not let it rest there. But, in pursuing the matter further, they have come full circle *(15, 26)*. And by this time the man is getting just the slightest bit exasperated: *'"I have told you already and you did not listen. Why do you want to hear it again?"'* (27a). And then a thought occurs to him; whether mischievous or serious is open to question. Whichever, it is a delightful moment in the proceedings. I only wish I could have seen their faces when he asked them: *'"Do you want to become his disciples, too?"* (27b).

The response of the Pharisees is all too predictable. His question has certainly touched them on the raw (28). Far from being daunted by their insults, he responds to them with a simple logic that cuts through their intellectual pretentiousness (30-33). In doing so, he answers their question about Jesus' origin, which seems to be giving them so much trouble. He starts with the fact that *'he opened my eyes'*, and from that point his argument proceeds something like this. Such an action could happen only through the power of God; and, since God doesn't listen to sinners, it stands to reason that the man doing it must be a godly man. The opening of the eyes of a blind man just doesn't happen; so this must be a miracle. Therefore, the man who did this miracle must have come from God, because only God can do miracles.

Totally disarmed by the man's logical reasoning, and frustrated by their inability to out-argue this outcast, they resort to insulting him further, hiding behind their pompous authority, and invoking their ultimate sanction (34).

When we speak out for Jesus, we may lose friends, be sneered at or even persecuted as a result, just as this man was. But let us be encouraged by the knowledge that nothing can ever take away our salvation or separate us from the love of God (Romans 8:38, 39).

'He found him'

So here the man is, thrown out of the synagogue with all that implies, and all because he dared to speak about what had happened to him. But Jesus hears about it. And not only does He hear about it, but He goes looking for him (35). What a moving picture that conjures up. In the midst of His hectic schedule, Jesus has time to come right where that man is. He engages him in conversation, bringing him to the point of confessing his belief, acknowledging Jesus as Lord, and worshipping Him as God *(35b-38)*.

And that wonderful time He spent with Jesus, and all the spiritual development that took place in his life as a result only happened because he was persecuted. And when we, too, suffer because of our stand for Him, Jesus will draw near to us, commune with us and minister to us right where we are, as we worship Him. It is often in our most difficult times that we most powerfully experience the presence of God, and make the most spiritual progress.

Steps to belief

It is interesting to note the four steps to belief taken by the man born blind:

- Jesus is a man who healed him *(11)*;
- He acknowledges Jesus as a prophet *(17)*;
- He recognizes that Jesus has come from God *(33)*;
- He worships Him as Lord and God *(38)*.

All the research that I know of indicates that the vast majority of people who come to believe in Jesus and put their faith and trust in Him do so after taking a number of steps. Rarely does it happen that a person comes to faith on his first encounter with the Gospel.

I find this very encouraging, because most of the times when I share my beliefs with people, there seems to be little response. Yet I believe that the Holy Spirit is at work in their lives, drawing them to Him. There may need to be several more inputs of the Gospel before they finally come to full faith in Christ. That's one reason we need to take every opportunity that comes our way to share our faith with others. In that way, we are bringing them one step nearer to the cross. What a joy it is when we find ourselves helping them to take that last step on their journey to faith.

The blind seeing: the seeing blind

It is not clear whether the conversation recorded in verses 39-41 occurred immediately after Jesus' meeting with the man born blind or some time later.

Throughout His ministry, Jesus had many run-ins with the Pharisees, and this is one of them. Jesus frequently referred to them as people who claimed to see, but who were, in fact, blind: blind to the truth that salvation did not come by keeping every single one of the Jewish laws, as they taught, but rather by repenting of sin and asking God for forgiveness.

The outcasts of society, who were blind to God's ways and were guilty of breaking His laws, are having their eyes opened by receiving Jesus' teaching, are repenting, and coming into his Kingdom. Whereas those, like the Pharisees, who thought they had already discerned God's ways, are becoming blind to the truth that Jesus is bringing by closing their eyes to it. This teaching about God's love, mercy and grace as the only means of salvation was totally foreign to what they thought they saw in the Jewish Scriptures.

May our eyes always be open to see what God is teaching us through His Word, and may we never come to it with our vision restricted owing to any preconceived ideas.

CHAPTER ELEVEN

SABBATH BREAKER

[Two people healed on the Sabbath]

1. Luke 6:6-11 (also Mark 3:1-6)
2. Luke 13:10-17

Introduction

In chapter 10 we saw how the Pharisees objected to Jesus' healing people on the Sabbath, because they classed such an activity as 'work', which was forbidden. Interestingly, however, medical attention was allowed on the Sabbath, but only in life-and-death situations, which does not include the incidents we are looking at.

1. The man with the shrivelled hand

Think before you think

The Pharisees were determined to build a case against Jesus to discredit Him in the eyes of the people, and ultimately to get rid of Him permanently. So, almost everywhere Jesus went, there was a group of them watching Him closely, marking His every word and action *(7)*. Sometimes they stayed in the background; on other occasions they confronted Him directly, usually asking Him tricky questions, which they hoped would catch Him out.

I can just see them huddled together, sitting at the back of the synagogue that Sabbath day, listening carefully to every word Jesus said as He taught the people *(6)*, hoping He might say something that they could use against Him, as they *'watched him closely to see if he would heal on the Sabbath' (7b)*.

The Pharisees hadn't said a word, *'But Jesus knew what they were thinking' (8a)*. As the Psalmist says: *'you perceive my thoughts from afar' (Psalm 139:2)*. Before God, we are an open book. We may be able to fool other people, but we can't fool God. He knows what we are thinking, and why we are thinking it. We can't hide anything from Him, however hard we might try.

Doing what is right

Jesus never shied away from confronting an issue. He was always meek, but never weak. He didn't allow Himself to be deflected from doing what was right by the presence of those who might disagree with Him or be upset as a result of His actions. He even healed people on the Sabbath, irrespective of the consequences.

It is sometimes difficult to follow that principle, and on those occasions we need to ask God for the strength, wisdom and courage always to do what is right in His sight. Being a member of the Kingdom of God and a child of our Father places an obligation on us to do what He says. This may not do a lot for our popularity rating in the world, but it is these sorts of situations that show whether our lifestyle and attitudes have really changed as a result of accepting Christ as Lord of our lives.

Perhaps we should ask ourselves the same question as the apostle Paul addressed to himself: *'Am I now trying to win the approval of men, or of God? Or am I trying to please men?' (Galatians 1:10)*.

Up-front obedience

It's at this point that I feel rather sorry for the man with the shrivelled hand. A feature of the three incidents we are looking at where Jesus healed on the Sabbath [including the man born blind] is that the people concerned do not ask Jesus to heal them, although they are still required to show their faith.

There's this man, sitting quietly minding his own business,

when suddenly he finds himself the centre of attention in the synagogue. And up-front too: not hidden away in the congregation somewhere *(8b)*. You've certainly got to admire his trust and obedience as *'he got up and stood there' (8c)* in response to Jesus' command, when running out of the place at a high rate of knots might have seemed a much more attractive proposition.

God always honours and blesses us when we are obedient to His word spoken into our lives. There may be times when we do not understand why God has commanded us to do something, or when we don't particularly want to do what God has told us. I'm sure the man in the synagogue experienced both of these reactions simultaneously: but he still obeyed and trusted God, and received the blessing of healing as a result. Learning to trust God develops as we walk with Him day by day and get to know more about Him. The hymn writer John Henry Sammis (1846-1919) put it like this:

> *When we walk with the Lord in the light of His word*
> *What a glory He sheds on our way!*
> *While we do His good will, He abides with us still,*
> *And with all who will trust and obey.*
> *Trust and obey, for there's no other way*
> *To be happy in Jesus, but to trust and obey.*

Silence was the reply

So, there the man is, standing out at the front, wondering what's going to happen next. Jesus ignores him for a moment, and turns His attention to the rest of the congregation, especially that little huddle on the back row, to whom in particular He addresses this question: *' "I ask you, which is lawful on the Sabbath: to do good or to do evil, to save life or to destroy it?" '* *(9)*. *Mark* tells us that *'they remained silent' (3:4b)*.

Jesus has pre-empted the Pharisees by asking them a question, a technique He uses from time to time. They can hardly say that doing evil or destroying life is lawful on any day, let alone on the Sabbath; but on the other hand they can't say the opposite is true either, because this would vindicate what

Jesus is doing by healing on the Sabbath. He asks them a similar question when He is about to heal a man from dropsy *(Luke 14:2-6)*. On both occasions, they find themselves in awkward positions, and, not for the last time, they refuse to answer the question.

Mark tells us that Jesus' reaction to this lack of response is one of anger and distress *(5)*: anger that they are giving the rabbis' rulings in the Mishna greater authority than the God-given Torah; distress at their stubborn refusal to accept that their thinking was wrong. The command to do no work on the Sabbath, which was stated in the Torah *(Exodus 20:8-11)*, was never intended to prevent good being done on that day. Its purpose was to grant all God's children time both to worship God and to enjoy the necessary rest and recreation required to recharge their batteries after a busy week. In effect, the Pharisees had placed these rulings about what was and what was not 'work' above the Torah, and thereby distorted the original intention of this commandment. Jesus was not a Sabbath breaker as the Pharisees maintained. He was, in fact, interpreting the Law about the Sabbath correctly and as God had originally intended. No wonder Jesus is angry and distressed.

Furiouser and furiouser

Now Jesus turns His attention back to the man waiting patiently and nervously at the front. *'"Stretch out your hand"' (Luke 6:10a)* He commands him. This is the moment of truth for the man. And, as we saw in the case of the paralysed man [chapter 7], it is as he overcomes any doubts that he might have, is obedient to Jesus' command, and puts his faith into action, that the healing begins, continues, and is completed *(10b)*.

The Pharisees are *'furious' (11a)* because Jesus has challenged their authority head on, and has shown up their reasoning for the foolishness that it is. They have no intention of putting up with this, and begin *'to discuss with one another what they might do to Jesus' (11b)*. *Mark* tells us that they even go to the extent of plotting with the Herodians *(3:6)*. Normally, religious groups like the Pharisees would have nothing to do with political groups like the Herodians. The Herodians were a pro-Roman Jewish party, who probably saw Jesus as a potential leader who might pose a threat to the political stability of the area, which they desperately wanted to maintain. So these two unlikely bed-fellows are prepared to sink their huge differences and unite against Jesus, the common enemy *(Mark 12:13)*.

2. A crippled woman

Pharisees rule OK?

Once again, Jesus is *'teaching in one of the synagogues' (Luke 13:10)* on the Sabbath. Each synagogue had a ruler, whose responsibilities included conducting the services, overseeing the worship, inviting people to take part in the services, and generally keeping order, besides carrying out various admini-strative functions.

Such rulers were usually laymen, and almost always Pharisees. It is interesting then that Jesus, whom they opposed, was given several opportunities by them to teach in the synagogues. Perhaps they felt that, since it was common practice and courtesy to invite itinerant rabbis to speak in the synagogue on the Sabbath, they could hardly exclude Jesus from this custom: besides the fact that a riot might have resulted among the people if they had. Or maybe it was part of their strategy of giving Him enough rope to hang Himself with, so to speak.

The power and the glory

Jesus notices a crippled woman in the congregation *(12a)*. Whether this was while He was in full flow, or when He had completed His teaching, we don't know. *Luke* tells us that she *'had been crippled by a spirit for eighteen years. She was bent over and could not straighten up at all' (11)*.

At the time of Jesus, various illnesses, both mental and physical, were attributed to the work of evil spirits, behind which was Satan, the source of all evil. The Bible shows quite clearly that everything God created was good *(Genesis 1)*, but when mankind chose to rebel against God evil came into the world with all its consequences *(Genesis 3)*, one of which was illness in all its manifestations.

Healing was one of the ways that Jesus showed His power over Satan and evil, foreshadowing the time when He will return, this time in all His glory, ushering in a *'new heaven and a new earth' (Revelation 21:1)*, when the original perfection of God's creation will be restored in full measure, so *'There will be no more death or mourning or crying or pain, for the old order of things has passed away' (21:4)*. What a wonderful place heaven is: and that is our destination, made possible by Jesus' triumph on the cross over sin and death and hell and all the works of Satan.

Saved and healed, restored and forgiven

In the Greek language, in which the New Testament was originally written, the word for healing and the word for salvation are one and the same. The Greek word 'Soter' means both 'Healer' and 'Saviour', and the word 'soteria' means both 'healing' and 'salvation'. In *Acts 14:9*, the Greek word 'sozo' is translated 'healed', and in *Romans 10:9* it is translated 'saved'. The Greek words for 'salvation' and 'saved' mean both spiritual and physical healing.

When Jesus died on the cross, it was so that we might be saved from the consequences of our sin, and so that the rift between ourselves and God caused by our sinfulness might be healed. The prophet Isaiah describes it beautifully: *'But he was pierced for our transgressions, he was crushed for our iniquities; the punishment that brought us peace was upon him, and by his wounds we are healed' (Isaiah 53:5)*. This makes it possible for us to be forgiven and restored to a right relationship with God: the relationship that God originally intended us to have with Him when He created us.

Assurance policy, with praise dividends

Jesus calls the woman to come to Him, speaks to her, and

then places His hands on her *(Luke 13:12, 13)*. It is interesting that He does it that way round. He tells her that she is healed before she can see any evidence of healing.

There are times when God gives us an assurance that things are going to happen before there are any real signs of anything actually taking place. In this way, our faith is developed and strengthened as we trust in God's word, and then see it confirmed. The greatest assurance we have is that we are saved, are being saved, and will be saved. The fullness of this awaits us in heaven. As the hymn writer Fanny J. Crosby put it:

> *Blessed assurance, Jesus is mine!*
> *Oh, what a foretaste of glory divine!*
> *Heir of salvation, purchase of God,*
> *Born of His Spirit, washed in His blood.*
> *This is my story, this is my song,*
> *Praising my Saviour all the day long.*

Notice that the healed woman *'praised God' (13b)*. Giving God the glory for what He has done is very important for two reasons. Firstly, because it acknowledges that what has occurred is all of His power and grace, and is not something we have deserved or merited. Secondly, because it gives testimony to the fact that God is at work today, and this personal witness draws other people to Him.

Unrighteous indignation

It is at this point that the synagogue ruler decides to intervene. In complete contrast to the woman, who is probably still praising God, maybe even singing or dancing for joy, he butts in and tries to throw cold water over what's happened. Unfortunately, in my experience, it seems often to be the case that whenever God moves in a miraculous way or ministers by the power of His Spirit in His Church there are people who will seek to belittle or explain away what God has done, rather than praise Him and give Him the glory.

It's easy to see why the synagogue ruler is feeling *'indignant' (14a)*. He's the one who's invited Him to speak, and here is Jesus taking advantage of the situation to the point of doing something which the Pharisees see as being illegal. He's afraid that things might get out of his control, and so he seeks to impose his authority on the situation. He is not prepared to allow Jesus to have His way among this congregation.

How careful we must be not to make the same mistake of quenching the moving of the Holy Spirit among us when we meet together, because we are fearful of what might happen if we let God take control and have His way among us. The apostle Paul pleads with us: *'Quench not the Spirit'*, but at the same time *'Test everything' (1 Thessalonians 5:19 KJV, 21a)*.

In my experience, when the Spirit truly comes there is order, not chaos; there is liberty, not licence; there are spiritual manifestations, not fleshly ones; there is reality, not sham; there is participation, not alienation; there is emotion, not emotionalism; there is excitement, not excess; and everything, absolutely everything that happens uplifts the name of Jesus and no one else's, and results in worship and glory being given to God alone.

Get your act together

The synagogue ruler completely ignores Jesus, and speaks directly to the congregation: *' "There are six days for work. So come and be healed on those days, not on the Sabbath" ' (14b)*. Who exactly he thought was going to come and heal them during the coming week when Jesus had moved on, I'm not sure. I don't think he thought it through to that extent. He just seems to be trying to score religious points and to reassert his authority.

Jesus answers him in the plural because his objections reflect the thinking of the Pharisees as a whole *(15a)*. The term 'hypocrites' is one Jesus often uses to describe them. The word is a theatrical term, and actually means a masked actor. Nowadays, the faces of actors can be altered dramatically by the use of make-up and other devices. In the past, such techniques were virtually unknown. So what an actor did was to hold a painted mask of the character's face, usually on a short stick, in front of his own. In this way, he could pretend to be someone he was not. And this was Jesus' constant complaint against the Pharisees. They said one thing, and did another. They put on an act in public, which was not borne out in private *(Matthew 23:25-28)*.

It is very challenging to consider how we measure up to this test. Are our words and actions in harmony, or is there a discord? Does the image we present in public square with the way we conduct ourselves in our private lives? Is the verdict of the God who sees all and knows all the same for us as it was for the Pharisees? A common taunt directed at the Church today is that it is full of hypocrites. May God help us to get our act together and to live lives of integrity that are pleasing to Him. Only then can we be effective ambassadors for Christ in the world in which we live *(2 Corinthians 5:20)*.

Loosed

Jesus takes the ruler to task, because on the one hand the Pharisees are happy for their animals to be loosed on the Sabbath in order that they might drink *(15)*, but on the other hand they are unhappy for a woman to be loosed from her illness on the Sabbath in order that she might live life to the full *(16)*. They place the welfare of animals above the far greater needs of people, and for this they are condemned by Jesus, and stand humiliated before the people *(17)*.

We are all crippled by sin, and our lives and the society which we have created are deformed as a result. Jesus came to set us free from the bondage of sin, just as He loosed this woman from her crippling deformity. Our deformed society can be reformed only if we as individuals are first of all loosed from the bondage of sin that binds us. No number of good intentions, focus groups or changes in the law, commendable as they all may be, can bring about that reformation. It starts with us as individuals. The reformation begins in our hearts.

CHAPTER TWELVE

A MAN WITH AUTHORITY

[The healing of the centurion's servant]
Luke 7:1-10
(also Matthew 8:5-13)

Introduction

We now come to two miracles, both involving Gentiles [people who are not Jews], who beseech Jesus on behalf of someone else. On both occasions, Jesus responds by healing those persons without ever seeing or meeting them. The first of these miracles involves a Roman centurion and his servant.

Rome rule

A centurion was a military officer in the occupying Roman army. As the word implies, he was in charge of a company of a hundred soldiers. Not surprisingly, most of the Jewish people hated the Romans, resenting their presence and the strict control with which they ruled. Some went beyond resentment and formed themselves into terrorist groups, the most notable of which was the Zealots. They were committed to driving the Romans out of Palestine by force, and acts of terrorism were part of their campaign.

This particular centurion lives in Capernaum, and he has a servant whom *Luke* tells us he *'valued highly'*, but *'was sick and about to die' (2)*. *Matthew* expands this by saying that the servant was *'paralysed and in terrible suffering' (8:6)*. The centurion has heard of Jesus and the miracles that He has been doing, so he decides to make Jesus aware of the situation regarding his servant.

Overcoming obstacles

Throughout this incident we cannot help but be impressed by the centurion's humility. He is a man of power and status, a representative of the mighty forces of Rome; a cut above all other races. And yet he humbles himself before this Jewish itinerant preacher. Whatever will his household think? Whatever will his fellow officers have to say about it?

There are many barriers that can stop us from coming to God. Pride and self-sufficiency can often hinder us. Admitting that we are sinners in God's sight and realizing we need a Saviour is a very humbling experience, but it is essential if we are to be forgiven and accepted into God's family *(1 John 1:8-10)*. Concern about what others may say or think is often an obstacle to coming to God. So is fear, which is probably why the sentences *'Fear not!', 'Don't be afraid!'* and *'Do not fear!'* occur over a hundred times in the Bible. And there are many more besides.

We need to identify the barriers in our lives, submit them to God, and ask for His strength and power to overcome them. Satan will put as many obstacles as possible in our way to stop us from coming to God and knowing His blessing in our lives. He does not want us to be in a full and flowing relationship with God, because he knows what can be achieved for God's Kingdom when we are.

Searching

Actually, this centurion's fellow officers probably wouldn't have been all that surprised, because they knew that he had gone out of his way to find out about the Jewish religion and to understand the culture and beliefs of the Jews. He had even gone to the extent of building a synagogue for them.

This makes me think that here is a man who is searching for the truth. Having failed to find it in the various religions he has met during the course of his service across the Roman Empire, he believes he has now found what he is looking for in Judaism.

God always meets with those who diligently seek Him. The people of Athens had altars to every god imaginable; and, in case they'd missed one out, they even had an altar bearing the inscription 'To an Unknown God'. They were engaged in a spiritual search. The apostle Paul seized on this during his visit there *(Acts 17:16-34)*, and explained how God wanted mankind to ' *"reach out for him and find him, though he is not far from each one of us. For in him we live and move and have our being"' (27b, 28)*. Be assured that if you are truly seeking God He will make Himself known to you. As the songwriter put it: *'He's only a prayer away'*.

Unworthy

All this has made the centurion very popular with the Jews in Capernaum. So much so, that the elders of the town are prepared to speak to Jesus on his behalf when he asks them to *(Luke 7:3-5)* – evidence indeed of the esteem in which he is held by the townspeople.

The fact that he sends the elders instead of going himself shows the deference and respect that he has for Jesus, even though he has never met Him. Also, he may have felt that, being a Gentile, he wasn't worthy enough to approach Jesus personally, and that Jesus would be more likely to listen to the Jewish elders than to him.

Of course, none of us is worthy enough to approach God. We are sinful; God is holy. But God has made it possible for us to approach Him. The writer of the epistle to the Hebrews explains how: *'We have been made holy through the sacrifice of the body of Jesus Christ once for all' (10:10)*. This means that we can *'approach the throne of grace with confidence, so that we may receive mercy and find grace to help us in our time of need' (4:16)*. What a wonderful privilege we have; what a wonderful promise is ours!

Undeserving

The Jewish elders were highly respected members of the

community, who combined the present-day roles of magistrate and town councillor, though they were not necessarily rulers of the synagogue. *Luke* tells us that when they found Jesus they pleaded earnestly with Him: *'This man deserves to have you do this, because he loves our nation and has built our synagogue' (7:4b, 5)*. So Jesus sets off for the centurion's house, saying: *'I will go and heal him' (Matthew 8:7)*.

The accounts of this incident recorded in *Matthew* and *Luke* differ in some respects, but only because *Matthew* characteristically abbreviates the miracle accounts, whereas *Luke* tends to give us more details. Luke, being a Gentile himself, wrote his gospel with Gentile readers in mind. Here, he is keen to emphasize the continued politeness and consideration that this Gentile centurion shows towards Jesus. This is why he puts his next words into the mouths of friends. It would seem more likely that the centurion would come to greet Jesus and speak directly to him at this point, which is how *Matthew* records it *(8:8-10)*. However, it's what is actually said that is really important.

Having studied the Jewish religion, including its customs and practices, the centurion knows that according to the laws of the rabbis, Jesus would defile Himself by going into the house of a Gentile, requiring a process of cleansing to be undergone as a result. That is why he says: *'"Lord, don't trouble yourself, for I do not deserve to have you come under my roof"' (Luke 7:6b)*. The elders might have thought that the centurion was a deserving case, but he knew better.

This serves to remind us that we are all undeserving of God's love, mercy and forgiveness. We can do nothing of ourselves to merit it, nor can we do anything to earn it: it is possible only through the grace of God. The apostle Paul makes this quite clear: *'For it is by grace you have been saved, through faith – and this not from yourselves, it is the gift of God – not by works, so that no one can boast' (Ephesians 2:8, 9)*. Jesus had to become *'sin for us' (2 Corinthians 5:21)* to bring about our salvation. He took our sins upon Himself, so that we could be made righteous and acceptable in God's sight: *'God made him who had no sin to be*

sin for us, so that in him we might become the righteousness of God'
(5:21). That surely is amazing grace.

Amazed

But it is what the centurion says next that causes Jesus to be amazed: *'But just say the word, and my servant will be healed'* *(Matthew 8:8b)*. Here is a man with authority and power recognizing a man with greater authority and greater power. Here is a man who realizes that his authority and power are temporal and of this world, but that Jesus' authority and power are eternal and not of this world. The similarity he sees between them is that both of them have only to command to be instantly obeyed. He knows that Jesus doesn't even have to see the person who needs healing: just to speak the word of authority is enough.

The centurion's grasp of the reality of the situation and his statement of faith which results leave Jesus *'amazed' (Luke 7:9a)*. So amazed, that He comments on the man's great faith to the crowd, commending it to them all by saying that He has not found such depth of faith anywhere among the Jews *(9b)*. These words would have been music to Luke's ears, as they showed unequivocally that Jesus responded to faith expressed by Gentiles just as readily as to faith expressed by Jews. The result is that the servant is healed immediately in response to the faith expressed by the centurion *(Matthew 8:13)*, and not because he in any sense deserved it as a reward for studying Judaism or building the synagogue, as the elders thought he might *(Luke 7:4, 5)*.

The irony is that Jesus *should* have been able to find such faith among the Jews. For centuries God, through their religious customs and practices and through the teachings of the prophets, had been preparing them for the coming of the Messiah, so that they would recognize Him and understand what He was doing when He came *(Luke 7:18-23)*. And here is this Gentile, with none of these advantages, having greater faith in Him than any of them.

Interestingly, Jesus is described as being 'amazed' on only one other occasion. That was when He was rejected by His own people in His home town of Nazareth, where He was *'amazed at their lack of faith' (Mark 6:6a)*. So here He was amazed on account of such belief, whereas at Nazareth He was amazed on account of such *un*belief.

A bit of a shock

Having commended the centurion's faith to the crowd, Jesus goes on to make some forceful points to them, but only Matthew records them. He is completely the opposite to Luke in that he is a Jew writing with Jews in mind. What Jesus says at this point probably wouldn't have made much sense to Luke's audience of Gentile readers, so he doesn't include it. Matthew, on the other hand, knows it's essential that his Jewish readers not only hear it, but understand its implications.

Jesus is saying that in heaven there will be those *'"from the east and the west"' (11a)*, in other words, Gentiles, sitting down at the feast *'"with Abraham, Isaac and Jacob"' (11b)*, the father figures of the Jewish nation, known as the patriarchs, each of whom showed great faith in God. But *'"the subjects of the Kingdom"' (12a)* represent the Jews who do not show faith in Jesus, the Son of God, and will therefore be excluded *(12b)*.

The fact that the Gospel is for the whole world is a recurring theme in *Matthew*, as seen in *28:19, 20*. The Jews should have known that when the Messiah came the salvation He brought would apply equally to the Gentiles as to themselves. The prophets whom God had sent to them down the years had made this quite clear. But it would still have come as a shock to those who regarded themselves as God's chosen people *(subjects of the Kingdom)* and therefore superior to the Gentiles, to be told that the other peoples of the world would be there in God's Kingdom, too. And, what's more, they were not going to be there as of *right,* just because they were Jews, as they had always assumed. They were going to be in God's Kingdom in heaven only if they, too, repented and put their faith and trust in Jesus.

Entrenched

The Jews were so entrenched in their religious traditions and ways of doing things that many of them found it impossible to accept Jesus and His message. It is important that we do not make a similar mistake in our churches: that of becoming so set in our ways that we cannot conceive how God can possibly work outside of them. The result of allowing this to happen is twofold. Firstly, we limit God to what He can do with us and among us. Secondly, when God does do something that is outside our preconceived structures, ideas and framework, not to mention our comfort zone, we dismiss it or fail to recognize His hand at work, and thus miss out on experiencing more of the blessing of God in new and different ways.

This is not to say that we should simply accept everything that comes along purporting to be 'in the Spirit'. It is important that everything be tested *(1 John 4:1)* and weighed in the light of God's Word. My prayer is that God by His grace will help us to get the balance right.

CHAPTER THIRTEEN

A DESPERATELY SEEKING MOTHER

[The faith of a Canaanite woman]
Matthew 15:21-28
(also Mark 7:24-30)

Bottom of the class

This is the second miracle where Jesus heals at a distance, and this time the supplicant is a Gentile woman. *Matthew* describes her as a *'A Canaanite woman' (22a)*, which *Mark* amplifies by telling us that she was *'a Greek born in Syrian Phoenicia' (26a)*. We have already seen in chapter 8 that women in those days were regarded as second-class citizens. A Gentile woman, who didn't even worship the one true God, was about as low as you could get in Jewish eyes. And yet, Jesus has time for her.

Jesus despises no one. Whoever we are, whatever our background or circumstances, however other people may regard us is of no significance in the eyes of God. Jesus welcomes us and has time for us. We are all equal in God's sight. As the apostle Paul puts it: *'For there is no difference between Jew and Gentile – the same Lord is Lord of all and richly blesses all who call on him.' 'There is neither Jew nor Greek, slave nor free, male nor female, for you are all one in Christ Jesus' (Romans 10:12; Galatians 3:28).*

Unfortunately, as *James* points out, the outworking of this principle was not always in evidence in the church then, and neither is it now *(2:1-4)*. To our shame, prejudice and discrimination are still apparent at times, and need to be addressed in the light of God's Word. The challenging and uncomfortable question is: How am I and my church reaching out to those who are poor, helpless, underprivileged and marginalized in our society? My prayer is that God will open our eyes to the opportunities that surround us.

Retire to Tyre

Jesus wanted to get away for a while from the opposition He was experiencing in the district of Galilee, to enable Him to spend some quality time teaching and talking with the disciples. So He left the north of Palestine and made for the coastal city of Tyre, which lay to the north west in the country of Phoenicia *(Matthew 15:21)*. Today, this country is called the Lebanon.

It is interesting that in both *Matthew* and *Mark* this incident takes place after Jesus has been explaining that what makes people 'unclean' is what comes from the heart and out of the mouth *(Matthew 15:18-20; Mark 7:20-23)*. Jesus now takes this teaching a stage further by going to the Gentiles, whom the Jews regard as unclean, to show that it is nothing at all to do with *who* people are or *where* they come from.

Jesus is Lord

This sorely distressed mother approaches Jesus, not subtly or sensitively but *'crying out, "Lord, Son of David, have mercy on me!"' (Matthew 15:22b)*. A Gentile she may be, but she recognizes and acknowledges both the Lordship and Messiahship of Jesus in words to be echoed later by Bartimaeus, words of which we have already considered the significance in chapter 9.

It is interesting that throughout their encounter the woman calls Jesus *'Lord' (22, 25, 27)*. The Greek word translated 'Lord' is 'Kyrios', meaning someone in authority. Like the Roman centurion [chapter 12], she realizes that Jesus has the authority to deal with her daughter's condition, and that He is in control of every situation. Both of them have an insight into who Jesus is which the Jews have failed to grasp.

The foundation of our faith is realizing exactly that: *who Jesus is.* It is shortly after this incident that Peter, speaking on behalf of all the disciples, acknowledges who Jesus is: *'"You are the Christ, the Son of the living God"' (Matthew 16:16).* This realization is what makes all things possible. It is not a matter of having great faith in God, but of having faith in a great God. It is on this rock of faith that the Church is built *(16:18)*. No wonder Satan tries to undermine the divinity of Christ, and often does it through the mouths of so-called leaders of the church, whose pronouncements on this subject, with some notable exceptions, inspire doubt rather than faith. There is a need in the pluralistic society in which we live to reaffirm clearly and unequivocally who Jesus is, the Son of the living God, rather than allowing Him to be reduced to the level of the founders of other religions and philosophies.

An anguished cry

Imagine the agony of this mother with a daughter who is *'"suffering terribly from demon-possession"' (15:22c).* She is obviously too embarrassed by her to bring her to Jesus. Her daughter is probably disruptive, even destructive, and a behaviour problem in society. It is quite possible that her husband has left her because of it, as it was unusual in those days for a woman to approach a rabbi. Usually it was the father, as in the case of Jairus's daughter and the epileptic boy [chapters 14 and 16]. Yet, in spite of the fact that the situation is driving her to distraction, she has not rejected her daughter, but continues to love her to the point of desperately seeking help for her. She has tried every avenue in the hope of finding a cure, but without success.

Few of us have experienced agony like that of this mother, but many of us have already coped, or will in the future have to cope, with heartbreaking situations concerning our own children. If there is one thing I have learnt over the years it is the importance of keeping on loving them, which is very tough going when you don't approve of what's happening or find it difficult to cope with. So often it would be much easier to reject them, and to live as if they don't exist. But the father in the parable of the Lost Son, also known as the Prodigal Son *(Luke 15:11-32)*, is the example that Jesus wants us to follow. Though it took many, many years, he never gave up hoping; he never gave up loving; and I'm sure he never gave up praying. And, when his son did finally return, he showed him nothing but compassion and forgiveness *(20, 22-24)*. That can't have been easy, but it is what God expects of us. And as we are willing to do that, and decide to carry it out, He will strengthen us, and enable us, and cause us to experience His love flowing through us.

Persistence pays

Unlike during His encounter with Bartimaeus, Jesus gives the woman no encouragement at all. He certainly doesn't have her brought to Him to ask her what she wants Him to do for her. In fact, *'Jesus did not answer a word' (23a)*.

This is the only time we see this in the whole of His ministry. Usually Jesus encourages people: here He seems to be discouraging the woman. Actually, I think He is paying her a great compliment. He knows the depth of her faith, but He wants everyone else to see it too. He knows that her faith is so sure that she will not be put off, but will persist until she is answered: just like the widow in His parable about prayer *(Luke 18:1-8)*. In the end, Jesus compliments her publicly *(28a)*.

And how persistent the woman is! The disciples get sick to the back teeth of her. So much so, that they *'came to him and urged him, "Send her away, for she keeps crying out after us"' (23b)*. Sometimes our faith is tested too. God just doesn't seem to be responding. How shall we react? Shall we ask just the once and then give up? Or shall we be like the child who, having set its heart on something, pesters its parents continually until it gets it? Advertisers have cashed in on the persuasive power of persistent children. And we as God's children need to show similar qualities of persistence in our prayers.

Jesus said: ' "Ask and it will be given to you; seek and you will find; knock and the door will be opened to you" ' (Matthew 7:7). But He didn't say how many times we would need to ask, seek and knock. In fact, the word 'seek' implies prolonged and intense activity, as exemplified in the children's game of 'Hide and Seek'.

If a parent initially refuses a child's request, it is often to see how important that particular desire is to the child. Is it just a passing fancy, or is it something more deeply rooted? If it's the latter, then it certainly won't be the last time the matter will be raised. And sometimes God wants to see, and also He wants *us* to see, how important that particular request actually is to us.

Worthy of worship

When Jesus does finally speak, it is to the disciples, and not to the woman, although He wants her to hear and understand the significance of what He is saying (24). He is making it quite clear that His mission is to the people of Israel, the Jews, and not initially to the Gentiles. This was because, as we saw in chapter 12, the Jews had been prepared by God for the coming of the Messiah, whereas the Gentiles had not.

This did not mean that Jesus would not respond to Gentiles who had faith in Him, but that the Gospel in all its fullness would not be made available to them until after His Ascension (Matthew 28:16-20). Still the woman is not put off. Her response is not doubt, or even huffiness, but remarkably it is worship: 'The woman came and knelt before him' (25a).

I find this very challenging. In the midst of the woman's desperation and distress, with her petition unanswered, she still comes to worship. How often is our worship or lack of it determined by our situation or circumstances? It is important to remind ourselves that God is worthy of our worship no matter whatever else may be happening or not happening (1 Thessalonians 5:18). Too often we are influenced by how we are feeling, by whether our prayers have been answered or not, or by the circumstances we find ourselves in. The result is that we do not worship God as we should, if at all.

The words of the prophet Habakkuk make the point beautifully: *'Though the fig tree does not bud and there are no grapes on the vines, though the olive crop fails and the fields produce no food, though there are no sheep in the pen and no cattle in the stalls, yet I will rejoice in the Lord, I will be joyful in God my Saviour' (Habakkuk 3:17, 18).*

The day of the dog

At last, Jesus replies directly to the mother's request for help. But He does it in rather a strange way *(26)*. The Jews called themselves the 'children of God', and often referred to the Gentiles as 'dogs'. Some say this was because, in the opinion of the Jews, dogs were just as likely to receive God's blessing as these pagan Gentiles were.

Jesus is making the point that the Gospel and all its blessings are first and foremost for the Jews, not the Gentiles. The woman, knowing that the Jews spoke of Gentiles in this way, cleverly extends the imagery. She clearly understands what Jesus is saying, and points out that the dogs take advantage of whatever comes their way *(27)*. In other words she is saying: Your priority may be the Jews, but you've come my way, Lord Jesus, and I'm taking advantage of that on behalf of my daughter.

And now, for the first time, Jesus speaks words of commendation and encouragement as He pronounces healing for the woman's daughter *(28)*. She takes Jesus at His word, and goes home expectantly. We can only imagine the transformation that occurred in that household on the day when the 'bread' became food for the 'dog'.

SECTION THREE

POWER OVER EVIL

CHAPTER FOURTEEN

THE CLASH OF THE KINGDOMS

[Jesus drives out an evil spirit]
Mark 1:21-28
(also Luke 4:31-37)

Mission statement

Significantly, this miracle comes almost immediately after Satan has tried to deceive Jesus into doing wrong by tempting Him to misuse His powers *(Mark 1:13; Luke 4:1-13)*. Having put the devil firmly in his place, *'Jesus returned to Galilee in the power of the Spirit' (Luke 4:14a)*, where He proclaims His un-equivocal mission statement: *'"The time has come . . . . The kingdom of God is near. Repent and believe the good news!"' (Mark 1:15)*.

'Good news' is what the word 'Gospel' means. On the following Sabbath, in His home synagogue at Nazareth, Jesus explains more about this good news. He says it's about freedom for the prisoners, recovery of sight for the blind, and release for the oppressed: and this will now begin to happen before their very eyes because *'"The Spirit of the Lord is on me"' (Luke 4:18, 19)*.

Jesus then spends the next three years going round Palestine putting this good news into practice. He frees those who are imprisoned by affliction, both physical and spiritual; the blind receive their sight, both in a physical and a spiritual sense; He releases those who are oppressed by Satan through exorcising demons. Thus people's lives are restored, and they are reconciled to God.

But Jesus' mission statement is too much for His fellow inhabitants of Nazareth: they can't handle it at all. They just can't believe that this Jesus, who has grown up from childhood in their midst, can possibly be a prophet, let alone the Anointed One, the Messiah. Their furious reaction drives Him out of Nazareth *(Luke 4:28-30)*; and from then on Capernaum becomes the centre of His ministry.

Sin city

Capernaum was a very wealthy city, but it was also very decadent and full of sin. It was the headquarters for many Roman soldiers, as we saw in chapter 12. The result of this was that the city was subject to pagan influences from all over the Roman Empire. It was certainly a place where the kingdom of Satan was well established, which made it a most appropriate setting for Jesus to demonstrate the power of the kingdom of God, which he had come to establish.

Not surprisingly then, as soon as He arrives on the scene, there is a clash of the kingdoms. And Jesus is quick to show His authority and supremacy right at the start of His mission. As the first epistle of John put it years later, maybe with this very incident in mind, *'The reason the Son of God appeared was to destroy the devil's work' (1 John 3:8b)*. He continued to destroy the work of the devil in the lives of many people in that city. And He continues to do that today through the power of the Holy Spirit at work in the world.

Ultimate authority

Jesus' teaching is enthralling the worshippers in that city synagogue. *Mark* tells us that *'The people were amazed at his teaching.' (22a)*. Why is this? They have heard many rabbis teaching in their synagogue. So what is different today? What is the reason for their fixed attention? The answer is *'because he taught them as one who had authority, not as the teachers of the law' (22b)*.

The people were used to going along week by week and hearing the rabbis arguing over the finer points of what the Law said. If a person asked them a question about the Law, they would usually quote a particular teaching, and back up what they had said by referring to what some other rabbi had stated in the past; a bit like lawyers do today. They did this to give their words more authority. 'Quibbling and quoting' is how Eugene Peterson in *The Message* describes what went on.

Jesus, on the other hand, does not do this. He doesn't spend His time arguing about nuances of meaning that are over the heads of most of the people. Nor does He quote what other teachers of the Law have said when He is asked a question. His authority is not based on support from other rabbis. He is the ultimate authority because He is God and knows perfectly well what the Scriptures say and what they mean. He is teaching them new things, and is teaching them with an authority that stems from God, who He is, not from whom He can quote.

A powerhouse or a talking shop?

And Jesus' authority is not a matter of talk: nor is it something conferred on Him by status. It is a matter of power: power such as He is about to demonstrate before their very eyes. The apostle Paul wrote: *'For the kingdom of God is not a matter of talk but of power' (1 Corinthians 4:20)*. And that applies just as much today as it did then. People respond when they see the power of the kingdom of God at work in the world, and that can happen only as we are prepared to allow the Holy Spirit to fill us and to flow out through us.

Unfortunately, in my experience, many churches are characterized by talk rather than by power. An indicator of this is often the numbers present at the business meeting compared with those attending the prayer meeting. In many cases we have become a talking shop rather than a powerhouse, with the result that our society is not seeing the kingdom of God in its fullness, which it should be able to do. People are drawn to God in many ways, but the most magnetic of these is when they see evidence of the power of God at work . My prayer is that God will so fill each one of us with Himself that we shall be a people who move in the power of the Spirit, thus bringing men and women to Christ.

Be quiet

We don't know whether Jesus has finished His teaching or not when the evil spirit manifests itself *(23)*. Sometimes mental illness is mistaken for demon possession and vice versa. Here is a clear case of demon possession, because the man reveals a knowledge of who Jesus really is. He is under the complete control of the evil spirit, which reacts violently to the authority of Jesus, crying out: *'"What do you want with us, Jesus of Nazareth? Have you come to destroy us? I know who you are – the Holy One of God!"' (24)*. The irony of this outburst is that the evil spirits know and acknowledge the true identity of Jesus, whereas the Jewish religious leaders, who should have recognized it, fail to see it or refuse to accept it.

It is interesting that, although the evil spirit is telling the truth about who He is, Jesus silences it. There are three main reasons for this. Firstly, He wants people to come to an understanding of who He is for themselves by listening to His words and observing His actions, not because some demon tells them. Secondly, He wants to reveal His Messiahship when He is ready, and not be pushed into it by Satan. Thirdly, Jesus considers the well-being of the man possessed to be paramount, so not only does He silence it; He casts it out *(25)*.

Some Jews thought that when the Messiah came He would destroy the demons. This would indicate that the kingdom of God had arrived. The evil spirit obviously knows this too *(24)*. Jesus also refers to it Himself on another occasion when the religious leaders accuse Him of driving out demons by the power of Beelzebub, another name for Satan or the devil *(Matthew 12:22-24)*. Having shown how ridiculous their argument is

(25-27), Jesus goes on to say: '"But if I drive out demons by the Spirit of God, then the kingdom of God has come upon you"' (28). And He leaves them to work it out for themselves.

A balanced perspective

Many in our so-called sophisticated and scientific society dismiss belief in evil spirits as pre-scientific explanations of mysteries that people in the past didn't understand: explanations that are totally inappropriate for today. Yet there is a great deal of evidence from both home and abroad that people can be and are possessed by demons, and need to be delivered by the power of God.

The danger is either to see demons everywhere, responsible for everything classed as bad, or to go to the other extreme and see them nowhere, responsible for nothing at all. It is important that we adopt a balanced perspective.

In my experience, demons cannot last for long in the presence of a holy God without manifesting themselves in some way, as happened here. And when they do show themselves, they need to be dealt with in the same way that Jesus did on this occasion (25). He binds the demon, forbidding it to speak, and then commands it to leave the man. I don't believe we should go looking for demons, but when they appear we must cover ourselves with the blood of Christ, and exercise the power and authority that we have over them in and through the name of Jesus. This authority was given by Jesus to His disciples (Luke 10:17-19), was carried on by the apostles after the Ascension (Acts 5:16; 8:7; 19:11-15; and particularly 16:16-18), and is also ours today (Mark 16:17, 18).

'Satan to Jesus must bow'

According to the Bible, evil spirits are actually fallen angels who are under the rule of Satan or Lucifer, an archangel who, in his pride and arrogance, rebelled against God and was thrown out of heaven (Matthew 25:41; 2 Peter 2:4; Jude verse 6; Revelation 12:7-9). They continue to seek to undermine, damage and destroy God's creation. They can tempt, afflict and oppress people, and where a person opens himself through any of the various occult activities, they can enter and ultimately possess that person. However, both Satan and his demons are subject to the power and authority of God. As the hymn writer put it: *'Jesus is stronger than Satan and sin; Satan to Jesus must bow'*.

This and several other confrontations throughout Jesus' ministry were but a pale foreshadowing of the conflict that would occur at the crucifixion. Then, Jesus would wrestle from Satan the keys of death and Hades *(Revelation 1:18)*, thus setting us free from these consequences of sin.

Christ's victory over Satan also means that people can be released from any harmful effects of being involved with the occult. Such experiences are more widespread than we may think, as people are sucked into the often fascinating and seemingly harmless world of evil. As a teacher of Religious Education in secondary schools for twenty-eight years, I discovered that hardly a term went by without some pupil or other seeking my advice about what could be done to free him from the nightmares or disturbances that had resulted from playing with a ouija board. I became increasingly concerned about what was happening, and was delighted when the Evangelical Alliance produced an excellent video on the subject of the occult called 'Doorways to Danger'. It examines many of the different entrances into the spirit world, including astrology, tarot cards, witchcraft, levitation, spiritism, and ouija boards. It warns of the dangers of becoming involved with any of these activities, but also emphasizes the fact that, because of what Jesus did on the cross, in and through His name we can be released from any evil affliction, oppression or influences that may have resulted from contact with the occult.

In my experience, it is essential that when people come to Christ they renounce any occult involvement and receive appropriate ministry. This renunciation includes getting rid of any occult literature, artefacts, symbols, clothing and anything at all that is connected with such activities. To follow the example of the people of Ephesus *(Acts 19:19)* may seem a little extreme, but in my experience it is very effective and helpful to the person as he turns his back on his old way of life and makes a new start in life following Christ. Failure to renounce occult involvement often results in deep spiritual problems, with the consequent lack of spiritual progress and growth in God. And having emptied himself in this way, it is vital that he allows God to fill him with His Holy Spirit, otherwise he may well find himself in an even worse predicament, such as Jesus Himself described *(Matthew 12:43-45)*.

Authority confirmed

The reaction of the people in the synagogue is understandable *(27a)*. We have already seen why they were amazed at His teaching, but now they have seen His authority confirmed in power. Giving orders to evil spirits, which the demons instantly obey *(27b)*, is also something new. Many so-called wonder workers of that day claimed to be able to exorcise evil spirits. They used spells, magic, and other involved processes: but Jesus simply speaks the word, and the effect is immediate. This is unheard of. What power! What authority! No wonder the news spreads throughout the region *(28)*. The kingdoms have clashed, and will clash again and again. But there will only ever be one Victor.

CHAPTER FIFTEEN

THE LEGION MEETS THE LORD

[Jesus heals a demon-possessed man]
Mark 5:1-20
(also Luke 8:26-37)

Gentile territory

As we noted in chapter 3, this journey across the lake *(1)* was not made just so that Jesus could get away from the crowds. There was a specific reason for it. Jesus was about to extend His ministry on to Gentile territory for the first time, having confined His activities to Palestine until then. Jesus wanted the Jews and everyone else to know that His mission statement included non-Jews as well, and that Gentiles were welcome in the kingdom of God. And He could have chosen no better way to demonstrate this than actually to venture into the Gentile *'region of the Gerasenes' (1)*. This was part of a larger area known as 'the Decapolis', which means 'the Ten Towns'.

It seems most likely that this incident took place in the area not far from the town of Gadara, which was about six miles inland. There was a rock wall near the shore, in which were a number of caves that were used as tombs. According to Jewish tradition, a tomb was one of the dwelling places of demons. And it was from a tomb that a deranged, demented demoniac emerged, and made straight for Jesus, who had only just got out of the boat (2).

Chains

The demoniac must have been a fearsome sight. I can imagine the disciples recoiling in terror as he gets nearer and nearer to where they are standing: a terror which keeps them firmly rooted to the spot. They can see that he is clad only in rags, with broken chains hanging from his wrists and clinging to his feet. As he approaches, they become aware that these rags are soaked in blood from the deep wounds caused by the chains, and from the self-inflicted cuts made with sharp stones. His hair is flowing, matted and bedraggled, and he has long since ceased to care about his appearance.

It had taken several of the local men to force him away from human habitation, and to hold him down while they fastened the chains to his wrists and feet in a futile attempt to protect themselves from him (3, 4). His superhuman strength came from the demons that possessed him. He might have been able to break free from the physical chains that bound him, but he was unable to break free from the spiritual chains that kept him in bondage to Satan.

We know that when we come to Christ, He sets us free from the chains of sin that bind us (John 8:36; Romans 6:17, 18). Yet it is possible for us still to be in bondage to Satan. There are all kinds of chains which he will use to restrict us, thus hindering us from serving God to the full, and being powerful and effective for Him in our daily lives. And it's so easy to fall into this kind of bondage. It can happen almost without our realizing it.

These chains can affect us mentally, emotionally, physically and spiritually. We can be bound by wrong thoughts and attitudes; by habits that we find so difficult to break, such as what we look at, what we read, where we go, what we spend our time doing, and what we put into our bodies, which are, in fact, 'a temple of the Holy Spirit, who is in you, whom you have received from

God' (*1 Corinthians 6:19*); by feelings of unforgiveness, bitterness, resentment and jealousy; by love of money, possessions, and the things of this world; by afflictions whose symptoms may be physical, but whose causes are not; by unresolved problems, whose roots lie somewhere in the past; by unrenounced occultic activities; by almost anything that Satan can use to chain us.

Through Jesus' death we can be set free, not only from the chains of sin but also from all the fetters with which Satan would seek to bind us. Remember that Jesus' mission statement includes these words: *'"He has sent me to proclaim freedom for the prisoners and . . . to release the oppressed"'* (*Luke 4:18*). Satan does not have the power to keep us bound. We can claim our freedom in the name of Jesus. And, having been set free, let's be vigilant lest we become enslaved once again. As the apostle Paul puts it: *'It is for freedom that Christ has set us free. Stand firm, then, and do not let yourselves be burdened again by a yoke of slavery'* (*Galatians 5:1*).

The tragedy of it

Rejected by the community who loathed and feared him, alone and desolate, the man runs aimlessly up and over the hills, in and out of the tombs *(5)*. What a tragic sight! How he came to be in this state we are not told. All we know is that he is now running frantically straight towards Jesus, who just stands there, waiting. In complete contrast to the disciples, Jesus is quite calm and has no fear or concern for His safety. He knows He is not about to be attacked.

The appearance of a group of people usually means another attempt to restrain the man, although this time it's different: they've come from the opposite direction, and by boat at that. Yet the demoniac does not run away from them; quite the reverse. Perhaps he is thinking that the best form of defence is attack, especially towards strangers. Maybe part of him somehow realizes that Jesus can help him. Or it could be a case of the demons propelling him towards the One they must submit to. Whatever is going on inside him, he arrives where Jesus is, and falls on his knees in front of Him *(6)*. Jesus immediately commands the demons to come out of him, which provokes the demoniac so much that he begins to shout *'at the top of his voice' (7a, 8)*.

Déjà vu

There is an interesting comparison to be made here. According to *Mark*, as soon as Jesus begins His ministry to the Jews, He is confronted by a demon-possessed man, as we saw in the last chapter. And, sure enough, as soon as Jesus begins His ministry on Gentile territory, Satan once again confronts Him. It is another example of the powers of evil being unable to cope with the superior power of the presence of God, and almost having to come out into the open, even though they know what the consequence will be.

Once again the evil spirit, this time speaking on behalf of all the others, recognizes Jesus' true identity, His divinity, and His power and authority *(7)*. Interestingly enough, this demon living in Gentile territory actually uses the title for God that only Gentiles used (see *Daniel 3:26)*. The superiority of Jesus' power and authority over it is such that the evil spirit is reduced to squirming before Him, pleading not to be tortured *(7b)*.

More than conquerors

Although we live in a world that seems to be in the grip of evil, we have no need to fear. God is sovereign: He is in control, and will ultimately deal with evil once and for all *(Revelation 20:10)*. Meanwhile, we can be victorious over anything that Satan brings against us, because Jesus triumphed on the cross. Having reminded us that *'Jesus is stronger than Satan and sin; Satan to Jesus must bow'*, the hymn writer I quoted in the last chapter continues: *'Therefore I triumph without and within . . . '*. The victory Jesus gained is complete in two respects. Firstly, it is complete because it was achieved once and for all. Secondly, it is complete because it allows us not only to triumph over the trials and circumstances which beset us from without, but also to triumph over the temptations and struggles that arise from within. We have all-round, all-embracing, all-encompassing victory in Christ over all the wiles of our defeated enemy.

The apostle Paul got very excited about this. Inspired by the Spirit, he contemplated Christ's victory, and wrote these wonderful words: *'If God is for us, who can be against us? . . . Christ Jesus, who died – more than that, who was raised to life – is at the right hand of God and is also interceding for us. Who shall separate us from the love of Christ? Shall trouble or hardship or persecution or famine or nakedness or danger or sword? . . . No, in all these things we are more than conquerors through him who loved us'* (Romans 8:31b, 34-37).

Power in the name

When meeting a class for the first time, my top priority as their teacher was to get to know their names as quickly as possible. I always drew up a class plan, and made them sit in the same places until I had got to know all of them. This meant I could address them individually and directly, thus avoiding any confusion. It was particularly important when it came to disciplining them: it was quite clear which one of them was coming under my power! By virtue of who I was, I had the authority to know their names so that I could deal with them effectively.

Jesus, by virtue of who He is, had the authority to know the name of the demon *(9a)*, so He could exercise His power over it and deal with it directly and effectively. The demon gave his name as 'Legion', saying that there were many of them *(9b)*. This emphasizes, if any further confirmation were needed, what a terrible state this poor man was in. A Roman legion consisted from three to six thousand men, and they were notorious for their violence and brutality. Whether the name was an indication of the actual number or the type of behaviour they caused is open to debate. What can be said with certainty is that however great the forces of evil are, Jesus has the power and authority to overcome them, as we have, in and through His name.

A pigtale

The demons begged Jesus not to send them *'out of the area'* *(10)*. They were afraid of being sent *'into the Abyss'*, as *Luke* puts it *(8:31)*. Instead, they asked Jesus if they could go into the herd of pigs feeding on the nearby hillside *(11, 12)*. This further emphasizes the fact that Jesus was in Gentile territory. Jews did not keep pigs: they were 'unclean' animals according to the Law of Moses, and were unfit for human consumption *(Leviticus 11:7)*. They weren't even supposed to touch them.

Jesus allowed the demons to go into the pigs, with dramatic results *(13)*. It wasn't that Jesus didn't care about what happened to the pigs. It was a case of the demoniac needing to be convinced that the evil spirits had been cast out of him, and that he had been delivered from the bondage of Satan.

It's hardly surprising that *'Those tending the pigs ran off'* *(14a)*, after the sights and sounds they'd just witnessed. And, human nature being what it is, *'the people went out to see what had happened'* *(14c)*, having heard the reports given by the herdsmen.

Released and restored

And when the people saw, they couldn't believe what they saw. *Mark* tells us that there were three aspects of the dramatic transformation of the demoniac that would have been difficult for the people to accept *(15)*.

First of all, the man was just *'sitting there'*, whereas they were used to his running all over the place, never still, always on the move; restless, twitching, panting. Secondly, he was *'dressed'*, whereas he was normally in various states of undress, clothes torn into rags. Thirdly, he was *'in his right mind'*, whereas usually he was either yelling at the top of his voice or grunting in an incomprehensible language, cutting himself with stones and behaving in a totally unpredictable manner. And yet, there he was, *'sitting there, dressed and in his right mind'* *(15)*. This seems to me to be a wonderful picture of each one of us when we accept Christ as our Saviour. Released from the bondage of sin, our relationship with God restored, we are welcomed into His presence and into His family. The three changes which were noticeable in the man can also be applied to us.

• *'Eirene'*

The first of these changes is that the man was *'sitting there'*, totally at peace. This speaks of the effect on our lives as we realize that, with the chains of sin broken, we are now at peace with God. No longer do we fear His presence or His judgement; the whole situation has been sorted. As the apostle Paul puts it: *'since we have been justified through faith, we have peace with God through our Lord Jesus Christ' (Romans 5:1)*. The Greek word for 'peace' is *eirene,* which actually conveys the sense of relief and rest that comes after a broken limb has been reset. If you've ever had that happen to you, as I have, then you'll know what an appropriate metaphor it is to describe the feelings we have on realizing that our relationship with God has been restored, and that we are no longer living under His judgement.

This change also speaks of the full commitment that marks discipleship. A rabbi's disciples would literally sit at his feet and listen to his words of wisdom, which they would often learn by heart and seek to live their lives by. The words of Jesus are far more than expressions of worldly wisdom. As Peter says when Jesus asks His disciples if they want to leave Him and listen to others: *'"Lord, to whom shall we go? You have the words of eternal life. We believe and know that you are the Holy One of God"' (John 6:68, 69)*. The challenging question for every one of us is this: Can the marks of discipleship be seen in *my* life?

• *Robes for rags*

The second change is that the man was *'dressed'*. This speaks of God's mercy and forgiveness towards us. *Luke* tells us that *'For a long time this man had not worn clothes' (8:27b)*, only rags; yet here he sits, clothed in a robe. We're not told where his clothing came from, but the fact that he was wearing it was evident to all.

The prophet Isaiah uses the idea of rags and robes to explain our situation before we receive God's forgiveness. He describes all the *'righteous acts'* we do to try to secure our own salvation as *'filthy rags' (Isaiah 64:6)*. But when he describes receiving God's salvation and forgiveness, he says that God *'has clothed me with garments of salvation and arrayed me in a robe of righteousness' (61:10)*. God has clothed us in garments of His own making, the cost of which was paid by His Son.

• *Transformed mind*

The third change is that the man was *'in his right mind'*. This speaks of a life that has been transformed. His mind has been renewed. His perspective on life has changed completely. He now has new attitudes, different values, and rearranged priorities. Once again we are challenged to examine whether in fact our whole perspective on life has been transformed since accepting Jesus as Lord and Saviour.

The apostle Paul says: *'Do not conform any longer to the pattern of this world, but be transformed by the renewing of your mind' (Romans 12:2a)*. Or as J. B. Phillips memorably renders it: *'Don't let the world around you squeeze you into its own mould, but let God re-mould your minds from within'*.

A missed opportunity

You'd have thought that the local inhabitants would be jumping for joy at what had happened, and praising God for ridding them of this nightmare. Not a bit of it! They just couldn't handle this amazing transformation at all; it blew their minds completely. They were used to the demoniac as he was. They had learnt to cope with his deviance, and to accept it as a part of their lives. They just stood there, gaping, asking themselves: What kind of power is this, that can transform a situation like this; that can bring peace into such turmoil; that can deal with such evil? Even though they had probably heard of Jesus' power already, and some of them might even have seen it at work before *(Matthew 4:25)*, when it had actually come where they were and dramatically affected their circumstances, they were afraid *(15b)*. Not grateful; not thankful; afraid. They didn't know what to think, let alone what to do. Their minds were in total confusion.

In their uncertainty, the people gather around the herdsmen, who had seen it all unfold before them on the shore below, and get them to go over the events once more *(16)*. What happened to the pigs seems to be the clinching factor. This stranger, they conclude, is obviously a dangerous man to have around. Whatever might He do next? And so *'the people began to plead with Jesus to leave their region' (17)*. They don't just ask Him politely: they beg Him to go, so afraid are they.

When Mark uses the word 'frightened' or 'afraid', it always means frightened in a religious or spiritual sense. The Gentiles gathered on that shore realize that something unbelievable and incomprehensible has happened that is outside their control. And that is the source of their fear.

What an opportunity they missed! What further miracles and wonders might they have witnessed had they embraced Jesus and welcomed Him into their villages and towns! But instead they allowed their fear of what He might do to dominate their minds, and they missed out on God's blessing as a result. What a tragedy it would be if we were to be guilty of the same kind of thinking in our churches!

Plan D

However frustrated Jesus may have been feeling by the response of the inhabitants of that region, He doesn't argue with them, or seek to persuade them otherwise. What graciousness He shows as He just gets back into the boat, ready to sail away *(18a)*. It's a sobering thought that our attitudes and responses can frustrate what God wants to do in our lives and in the life of the church.

As Jesus is getting into the boat, the man He has released and restored *'begged to go with him' (18b)*. He wants to spend his life in the company of Jesus, serving Him, learning more about

Him, growing as a disciple. But Jesus has other plans for him.

From the man's point of view, it must have seemed quite clear what Jesus would want him to do; but perhaps he is asking to go with Jesus for the wrong reasons. Maybe I do him an injustice, but what if his real motivation is to escape from this place, where for the rest of his life he will have to live with the shame of his past hanging over him? I couldn't blame him if it is. The thought of people pointing him out, sniggering behind his back, making rude comments, even avoiding him, may have been too much for him to cope with just then.

Sometimes it may seem obvious what God would have us to do. But before we go ahead and do it, let's make it a matter of earnest prayer, asking God to confirm it to us in some definite way, so that we know we are not doing it for the wrong reasons. It may be, as in this case, that God in His wisdom has something completely different planned for us: a divine plan.

To boldly go

Until this moment, Jesus has been telling those He has healed to keep quiet about what He's done for them, and not to go round telling everybody [see chapter 6]. But, as He is now among Gentiles, who have no tradition or concept of a coming Messiah, He can allow people to speak quite freely about Him, without concern for the consequences that could have ensued had He adopted such an approach back in Palestine. Obviously, the man would make an extremely effective witness to the power of Jesus, and to the love and mercy of God that was being extended even to the Gentiles.

I would imagine that the man is rather taken aback when he hears Jesus' Plan D (19). His family had probably disowned him long before, although they might have taken him food. Now Jesus is commanding him to go back home and tell them what God has done for him and how He has had mercy on him. Not only are they going to hear about the change: they are going to see it before their very eyes. And seeing it will open the way for them to hear about it.

I find it very challenging to reflect on whether people see the difference in me that God has brought about, or whether it's barely perceptible in my daily living. Is it attractive and noticeable enough for them to want to hear about what's happened in my life, and to desire the same experience of God for themselves? And when the opportunity arises, do I take advantage of it and speak out boldly?

I remember once having such an opportunity in the school staffroom, and although I did speak out, I did so rather hesitatingly and cautiously. Later that same day, I was taken to task by a non-Christian colleague who had been present. He told me that I had something to say that was important and well worth hearing, and asked why I was so apologetic about it. I was quite shaken by this, but also stirred. The result was that I purposed from that day forward to seize every opportunity with boldness.

Of course we need to be wise and sensitive about how, when, where, and with whom we share the Gospel, and not just go barging in, bashing people with the Bible. But I'm convinced that we need to be more proactive and positive in our approach to sharing our faith. And, as we do so, we know that God will give us the right words to speak as we allow ourselves to be guided by His Spirit, in whatever situation we might find ourselves *(Matthew 10:19, 20)*.

I wonder if we dare pray this prayer: 'Lord, give me an opportunity today to speak to someone about you.' The trouble with this kind of prayer, in my experience, is that God often answers it with an alacrity that I sometimes wish He would show in response to some of my other prayers! Which just serves to remind me of the importance God attaches to our fulfilling His Great Commission *(Matthew 28:18-20)*. And so often, as with the ex-demoniac, our witnessing begins at home, which can be the most difficult place.

Let's get personal

I'm always impressed by the man's obedience *(20a)*. He must be very disappointed to find that Jesus is not going to allow his request. Yet he doesn't make the sort of excuses that we are all aware of, and often use, as to why we can't possibly go and tell. And we realize that he has more reason than most to make excuses. This is especially the case as we bear in mind the situation that he is going to have to face in the community. Nor does he need to attend a host of seminars and evangelism training courses before he can successfully communicate the Gospel to people. It's a simple matter of personal testimony: *'Tell them how much the Lord has done for you, and how he has had mercy on you' (19b)*.

Personally, I have nothing against taking advantage of seminars and courses, provided that we become better witnesses for Christ and are stirred up to share the Gospel as a result. However, I can't help but think that we spend so much time learning about how to do it rather than actually getting on and doing it. And, in my experience, that applies not only to evangelism but to all areas of church activity. The most effective resource for effective evangelism is still the personal testimony of what God has done for me, how He has had mercy on me, and how my life has been transformed as a result.

And because of the man's obedience, the Gentiles of that region heard of the power and mercy of God, and *'were amazed' (20b)*. And I don't doubt that the result of their amazement was that many were brought into the kingdom of God, and in due course became part of the Early Church. My prayer is that we shall all have the same enthusiasm, as this man had, for sharing our personal testimony with others, despite the difficulties that we may have to cope with.

CHAPTER SIXTEEN

FATHER AND SON

[The healing of a boy with an evil spirit]
Mark 9:14-29
(also Matthew 17:14-20; Luke 9:37-43)

Back to reality

In all three gospel accounts, we see that this incident takes place immediately after the Transfiguration. Peter, James and John have been privileged to catch a glimpse of Jesus as the Son of God in His glory: an experience that has understandably overwhelmed them. They have experienced the light of the presence of God: and now they are about to experience once again the darkness of the presence of evil.

It would have made the contrast between good and evil all the sharper for them. And it is the same for us: the more aware we become of the presence of God, the more aware we become of the presence of evil. From the mountain-top experience, they are coming down to earth with a bump: back to the reality of living in this world. And how often are *our* mountain-top experiences so swiftly followed by valleys of darkness and difficulty?

Jesus returns to a situation where His disciples have been unable to cast out a demon *(18c)*, and are in the middle of an argument with the teachers of the Law *(14b)*. They may have been criticizing the disciples, and by implication criticizing Jesus, because they haven't been able to help the boy who is in desperate need. Then *Mark* gives us this lovely picture of the crowd's response as they are suddenly aware that Jesus has appeared on the scene *(15)*.

In response to Jesus' question *(16)*, the boy's father speaks up, and gives him a vivid description of his son's symptoms, and what he considers to be the cause *(17, 18b)*. The details he gives would suggest that the boy was subject to epileptic fits. This can be frightening enough today, when we know what's going on. So it is hardly surprising that in Jesus' day they believed that these fits were the attacks of an especially vicious demon. Jesus' subsequent actions show that it certainly was so in this case, but in my opinion it would be a mistake to draw the inference from this that epilepsy is caused by demon possession.

The disciples

The father certainly doesn't spare the disciples' blushes *(18c)*. Jesus has given them the authority to cast out demons *(Mark 3:15)*, and they had successfully done this when sent out on a mission *(6:13)*. But not here. This is obviously puzzling them, too, because later on in private they ask Jesus: *'"Why couldn't we drive it out?"' (28b)*.

Jesus' reply seems to suggest two things. Firstly, that there are different kinds of demons. Secondly, that the disciples need to be reminded not to take the power they have been given for granted, but through prayer to be in constant touch with God, who is the source of the power they need to be able to deal with all manifestations of evil. We, too, need to be reminded of the importance of constant prayer, in order that we may be ready at all times to deal with the work of the enemy, wherever we may come across it.

Some of the gospel manuscripts have the words *'and fasting'* at the end of verse 29. Many books have been written on the subject of fasting, so I will confine myself to this one point. Fasting is a physical sacrifice, which symbolizes the fact that we realize how important prayer is, and that we are earnest about the prayers we are making. It shows God that we really mean business with Him about this particular matter.

The people

Jesus has some particularly severe words for the Jewish people. He describes them as an *'unbelieving generation'* *(19a)*, and speaks in the same tone as God had done many times in the past as He criticized His people through the prophets, such as Jeremiah, for not putting their trust in Him *(Jeremiah 5:23)*. Apparently, one of the rabbis had actually said that the Messiah's generation would be characterized by its lack of faith and belief. Jesus' language here would seem to confirm that.

There is also an interesting parallel here with *Exodus 32-33:6*, where Moses has been talking to God on a mountain, and has also returned to find God's people behaving as though they have no faith.

Once again, we see the importance that Jesus attaches to corporate faith. This is not just a matter between Jesus and the boy's father, although that is a very important aspect, as we shall see. Jesus is looking for faith in the crowd, and He doesn't find it.

It is so easy for us to leave the task of praying for those needing healing of any kind to others, such as the leaders of the church. Certainly, they have a vital role to play *(James 5:14)*, but so, I believe, do the rest of us. In my experience, the power of God to heal is wonderfully released as God's people lift up His name in praise and worship, and join their faith together to pray for the sick and needy. None of us is a spectator: we are all involved together. This is part of our ministry to one another as the body of Christ. It is also pertinent to ask ourselves whether Jesus is experiencing the same kind of frustrations with us now as He clearly was with the people then.

The father

• *What doesn't happen next*

When Jesus commands the boy to be brought to Him, another fit immediately ensues. Again, it's as though evil cannot help but manifest itself in the presence of God.

I'm always surprised, amazed even, at what happens next:

or, more accurately, what doesn't happen next. Jesus engages the father in conversation, rather than getting right on with the business of dealing with the evil spirit. Jesus is obviously not satisfied with the fact that the father has brought his son for healing, and feels it's important to probe more deeply into the father's thinking. This, incidentally, is for the father's benefit, not His; Jesus already knows where the father is coming from.

• *Crucial conversation*

So Jesus conversationally asks the father: *'"How long has he been like this?"' (21a)*. The father, probably with one eye on his distressed son writhing about on the ground, explains that this has been happening since childhood, and with dangerous consequences at times *(21b, 22a)*. But it is the next clause he uses that is the one Jesus has been waiting for: *'"If you can do anything"' (22b)*. He picks it up immediately, and quotes it back at him *(23a)*. I don't think He does this in an indignant way, but rather with the gentle firmness that is characteristic of Jesus on so many occasions during His ministry. It's not a question of whether Jesus has the power to heal the son: it's a question of whether the father has the faith to believe that Jesus has the power to heal his son.

Jesus' compassion for the man is such that He is determined to strengthen his shaky faith, and give him solid grounds for putting his complete trust in Him. So He continues with these mind-blowing words: *'"Everything is possible for him who believes"' (23b)*.

What an encouraging statement that is for all of us. Everything is possible because we have an almighty God who can do absolutely anything. That doesn't mean to say, however, that – if we have faith to believe – our petitions will be granted. God answers our prayers as, when, and how He sovereignly sees fit. But what it does mean is that when we pray, we should do so with that assurance fixed firmly in our minds, setting no limits on what God can do, and not doubting for one moment that God is able and willing to deal with the situation.

- *Rapid response*

Thus encouraged by Jesus, the father's response is immediate *(24)*. All the years of pent-up emotion and anguish due to his son's condition come pouring out of him in this exclamation of faith, which is what Jesus has been waiting to hear. The Amplified Bible beautifully captures the father's passionate entreaty in its rendering of verse 24: *'At once the father of the boy gave an eager, piercing, inarticulate cry with tears, and he said, Lord, I believe! Constantly help my weakness of faith!'*

As a parent, my heart goes out to the man. He is desperate that any unbelief on his part should not prevent his son being healed. He wants him to be made whole more than anything else in the world. How often do those of us who are parents wish we could take the pain rather than see our children suffer? We cannot. But what we *can* do is to ask God to strengthen our faith, and, in an echo of the father's words, to help us 'overcome our unbelief', so that we keep believing for a miracle at the hands of the God for whom everything is possible.

We may be desperate concerning our children for reasons other than the physical: and not only our children, but other loved ones too. Let's continue to pray believing, faith-full prayers on their behalf, knowing that God is hearing and answering in His way and in His time.

The personal touch

For this father, the time has come. Jesus proceeds to deal with the evil spirit that is causing the fits in His customary way by just speaking the word *(25, 26a)*.

Notice the personal touch here. Most of the crowd thought the boy was dead *(26b)*, but Jesus knew better. Even so, He didn't just walk away and leave him to recover. He went over to the boy, and *'took him by the hand and lifted him to his feet, and he stood up'* *(27)*. That reminds us once again of God's loving care and compassion for each one of us. The gospel writers leave us to imagine the father's unconfined joy as he gathers his son in his arms, and the realization dawns on him that never again will the boy suffer in that way.

Childhood influences

The question remains: Was Jesus merely being conversational when He asked the father, *'How long has he been like this?'* *(21a)*, or was He attaching a particular significance to the issue of how the boy came to be in this state? Many would say the former, but if the latter were to be the case, then what can we learn from it?

It is possible that the boy's condition was hereditary, which makes renouncing any occult activity as discussed in chapter 14 even more important, lest our children be affected by it in some way. If the presence of the evil spirit was due to the boy's being influenced by or even involved in such practices when very young, then it serves as a warning to all of us who are parents to take a close interest in everything our children are involved with, and that includes what they read or watch on television, to avoid any spiritual harm coming to them. I am old fashioned enough to believe that we have the responsibility to exercise censorship in the best interests of our children, so that they may be protected from all the evil influences that are around today. I do not write these words to scare anybody, or to make anyone paranoid: just to make us vigilant, and to pray continually for God's protection upon our children, even if they are very young.

SECTION FOUR

POWER OVER DEATH

CHAPTER SEVENTEEN

THE WEEPING WIDOW

[Jesus raises a widow's son]

Luke 7:11-17

Death duties

As Jesus and His large following are nearing Nain, a town to the south of Nazareth, they meet a funeral procession coming out through the town gate, making for the cemetery *(11, 12a)*. It seems as if the whole town has turned out to support the bereaved woman in her time of grief *(12b)*.

Honouring the dead was very important in Jewish culture. The body of the deceased would be wrapped and placed on a bier, a sort of stretcher. As it was carried to the burial ground, the dead person's relatives would follow on behind the bier, and onlookers would normally join in the procession. If the family could afford it, hired mourners would weep and wail aloud, initially at the house of the bereaved, and then during the whole of the procession. There then followed thirty days of mourning, during which the family would usually stay at home. It became the custom for them to sit on low stools for much of the time as a symbol of how they were feeling. The Kaddish, a prayer for the dead, would be said in the synagogue, usually every week for eleven months.

The widow's plight

Imagine the contrast between the two crowds. The one with Jesus is happy, noisy, joyful, lively; the other is sad, silent, sorrowful, sombre. As the two draw closer together, realization gradually spreads through the crowd with Jesus, starting with those at the front, and the mood changes accordingly.

It is interesting that Jesus' only visit to Nain should coincide with this funeral. Which reminds me of how often coincidences seem to happen when we pray. Nothing that God does is coincidental: it is all part of His sovereign purpose.

This surge of sympathy for the woman is probably also due to the townspeople's understanding of the desperate predicament she now finds herself in. For the body that is being carried to the burial ground is not that of her husband, but of her only son *(12a)*. After the death of his father, the son would have supported his mother; but now he is dead she is left destitute and alone. At her age, she would be unlikely to marry again, and unless she has family who will take her in, her only means of survival will be through begging on the streets. What a tragic state of affairs. And then, suddenly, seemingly from nowhere, Jesus appears.

Times of tears

Throughout his gospel, Luke emphasizes Jesus' care, concern and compassion for the poor and needy. This included women, who, as we saw in chapter 8, were regarded as second class citizens. Here we have a lovely example of His care. Interestingly, the woman doesn't come and ask Jesus for help, nor does she display any faith. He knows what she needs, and doesn't even wait for her to ask.

Luke tells us that when Jesus saw this poor widow, weeping tears mingled with desperation, *'his heart went out to her and he said "Don't cry"'* *(13)*. To which her response might well have been something like: 'Don't cry! What do you mean, don't cry! You don't understand the situation I'm in at all. I'm destitute, totally bereft of all support, and my future just doesn't bear thinking about. And you're telling me not to cry! As far as I'm concerned, tears are all I've got left.'

When we find ourselves in a traumatic situation, it's so easy to be overwhelmed by the circumstances to the point where we are convinced that God just doesn't understand, and even find ourselves believing that He has forsaken us. Be assured that He does understand *(Job 23:10a)*, and that He will never forsake us *(Hebrews 13:5b, 6)*. Whenever God sees us in those times of tears, His heart of compassion goes out to us, and He comes to speak words of comfort and reassurance to us *(2 Corinthians 1:3, 4)*. And not only that: He wants to be actively involved with us, wiping our tears away and giving us His joy in place of our sorrow *(Jeremiah 31:13b)*. He is able to do this, for He is the Lord of every situation.

'Kyrios'

And that is exactly the title Luke uses of Jesus here *(13a)*. He is reminding us that Jesus is well able to do something miraculous in the life of this woman and in the death of her son.

The Greek word for 'Lord' is *Kyrios,* and it is interesting that among the gospel writers only Luke makes frequent use of it. It is used of people who have authority, but it means more than simply the fact that Jesus has authority. The Old Testament, as we call it, was originally written in Hebrew. In that language, God's name was 'Yahweh'. As the Jews began to understand the holiness of that name, they ceased to pronounce it, as a way of acknowledging how holy it was. Instead, they began to use the title 'The Lord'.

Owing partly to the conquests of Alexander the Great, Greek became the language spoken by everybody in the countries around the Mediterranean Sea. That is one of the reasons why the Old Testament was translated into Greek. This translation became known as 'the Septuagint', and in it the word *Kyrios* was used for God's name.

The early Christians, particularly those who were Gentiles, used the Septuagint, and would therefore know that *Kyrios* was a title for God. That is why Luke, a Gentile himself, writing his gospel especially so that Gentiles could understand who Jesus is, calls Him *Kyrios:* the Lord; God Himself. And, as he has recorded earlier in his gospel: ' *"Nothing is impossible with God"* ' *(1:37)*, as this weeping widow is about to discover in a most dramatic way.

Surely not

Meanwhile, the bier is still being processed to the place of burial, so Jesus strides up to it and touches it, with the result that *'those carrying it stood still' (14a)*. They were probably completely taken aback that anyone would do such a thing, because touching a coffin made a person religiously unclean. But, once again, Jesus is not interested in the consequences for Himself: His only concern is for the widow.

Now everyone in both crowds has stopped and is watching intently. The people from the town have no doubt heard about Jesus, but they might not have realized that this is actually He in person. 'What is that crazy man doing?' they were probably asking themselves, though hardly daring to whisper it to their neighbours.

Many of the people who had come with Jesus, especially the disciples, had seen Him demonstrate His power over nature, over illness and over evil: but never over death. Surely not. He can't be going to . . . . And so they watch, open-mouthed, catching their breath, hardly daring to move.

Son alive!

Once again, Jesus speaks the word of authority, and demonstrates His power over death for the first time *(14b, 15)*. Even death must release its grip at Jesus' command. Imagine the reaction of the coffin bearers when the dead body that they have been carrying suddenly sits bolt upright and begins to speak. I'd love to know what he said, but unfortunately Luke doesn't tell us.

And as for his mother: what must her reaction have been? Probably shock and joy in equal measure. She's apparently rooted to the spot, because *Luke* tells us that *'Jesus gave him back to his mother' (15b)*. For me, this conjures up the lovely picture of Jesus helping the young man down from the bier, as the coffin bearers stand there completely dumbstruck, and ushering him into his mother's outstretched arms for the biggest embrace anyone would ever be likely to see!

Threefold response

The response of the people to this amazing miracle is threefold: awe, praise, and belief *(16)*. What they have just seen is totally awesome, filling them with wonder at the mighty power of God demonstrated before their very eyes. And what they have seen with their eyes evokes almost involuntary praise from their hearts. This in turn strengthens the belief in their minds that once again God has come among them to help them, although their understanding is limited for the moment to thinking of Jesus as a prophet.

Because Christ proclaims God's message boldly, performs miracles, and has now raised the dead, the people are beginning to equate Him with the prophets Elijah and Elisha, both of whom had been involved in bringing children back to life *(1 Kings 17:17-24; 2 Kings 4:18-37)*. They have yet to grasp the significance of the fact that both Elijah and Elisha cried out to God on these occasions, whereas Jesus just spoke the word of authority. This means He is much more than a prophet; this means He is greater than Elijah or Elisha; this means that Jesus is God Himself.

The economy of God

What encouragement there is for us in this miracle, and what an important lesson there is for us to learn. However desperate our situation may be, God is right there with us. And, as we commit it to Him, He will always bring blessing for us into it, and bring glory to His name out of it. He may not always perform the miracle we might want, but He will certainly minister His supernatural power, strength, courage, peace, wisdom, or whatever else it may be that we need, if we ask Him; and that in itself is a miracle of divine grace.

I don't believe that God, who is love *(1 John 4:8)*, deliberately causes us to go through bad experiences or brings traumatic happenings into our lives to teach us something. However, I do believe, as we submit every situation that we go through to God, no matter how devastating it might be, that He will wonderfully use it to draw us closer to Himself, to help us learn more about Him, to give us opportunities for witness that wouldn't have occurred otherwise, to enable us to minister more effectively to others as a result of what we've been through, and for many other purposes.

When I was at university, there was a student who had been seriously injured in a road crash, and as a result would be confined to a wheelchair for the rest of her life. Yet she just radiated the love of Jesus and the joy of the Lord to everyone she met, and her commitment was an example to us all. The fact that she had no bitterness towards God because of her accident was something that most of her fellow students just couldn't understand, and this made her a much more effective witness than the rest of us put together. She had so many opportunities to testify as a result of her disability, and was a source of comfort to many.

To me, she is an excellent example of the fact that nothing, but nothing is ever wasted in the economy of God. We just need to allow Him the opportunity to recycle it.

CHAPTER EIGHTEEN

DEATH OF A DAUGHTER

[Jesus brings Jairus's daughter back to life]

Mark 5:21-24, 35-43

(also Matthew 9:18, 19, 23-26; Luke 8:41, 42, 49-56)

Dynamic demonstration

It is interesting to note that this particular incident comes at the end of a sequence of miracles in which Jesus first of all shows His power over nature *(Mark 4:35-41)*, then His power over evil *(5:1-20)*, followed by His power over illness *(5:25-34)*, and now His power over death *(5:21-24, 35-43)*: a wonderful, dynamic demonstration of His supernatural power over anything and everything.

Whenever my faith is in need of a boost, this is the section I read as a glorious reminder that there is nothing that comes my way with which God in His supernatural and sovereign way cannot deal.

Another interesting point is that the three people Jesus ministered to in these miracles were all considered 'unclean' in Jewish society, and were to be avoided. But the compassion of Christ reached out to them and restored them.

Do you see the Pharisee?

Having returned across the Sea of Galilee from the region of the Gerasenes, Jesus very likely is back in Capernaum. He hasn't been there long before something happens which makes the people of the city wonder if they can actually believe their eyes.

Through the crowd comes Jairus, one of the rulers of the local synagogue. Presumably he's come to challenge Jesus on a point of law: this was the usual reason why such a Pharisee spoke to Jesus from time to time. But no! Jairus doesn't look like a man who's intent on a discussion: just look at his face. There are tears in his eyes. He's prostrating himself at Jesus' feet. Can you believe it? One of the Pharisees flat on his face before Jesus. What's going on?

Their silent question is soon answered, as the Pharisee raises himself to look up into the face of Jesus. He pleads *'earnestly'* with Him: *'"My little daughter is dying"' (23a)*. *Luke* tells us that she was his only daughter and was twelve years old *(8:42a)*. Gasps all round the quietened crowd. *'"Please come and put your hands on her so that she will be healed and live"' (23b)*.

The measure of the ruler

I'm always impressed by Jairus's humility, courage and faith. A man of status in the community, he overcomes both his pride and his fear of what others, such as his fellow rulers, will think of him and say about him, and publicly humiliates himself before this teacher from Nazareth. That is the measure of the man.

It's challenging to ask ourselves how well we measure up against the yardstick of humility. Sometimes we can be too proud to come to God, considering it a reflection on our lack of self-sufficiency. Sadly, God can do nothing for us until we acknowledge our need of Him, however humbling an experience that may be.

Sometimes God cannot use us because we have a proud spirit that is prepared to serve God only in certain ministries, and not in those we consider to be beneath us. I heard of a senior minister in London who used to take anyone being considered for a leadership position on a walk round the church grounds. Empty beer bottles, drink cans and all sorts of litter were often thrown in there over the wall. Any candidate who didn't stop to pick up at least some of the refuse was considered to be lacking the necessary humility to measure up to the requirements for and responsibility of leadership.

Jesus Himself is, of course, the supreme example of humility. The apostle Paul challenges us to be like Him with these words: *'Your attitude should be the same as that of Christ Jesus: Who, being in very nature God, did not consider equality with God something to be grasped, but made himself nothing, taking the very nature of a servant . . . he humbled himself and became obedient to death – even death on a cross!' (Philippians 2:5-8)*.

Faith at last

True, Jairus was driven by desperation, but, nevertheless, what he did took enormous courage for a Pharisee, as it was tantamount to treason. And what faith he had. Presumably it stemmed from what he had seen the previous Sabbath in his very own synagogue, when Jesus had cast an evil spirit out of a member of his congregation *(Mark 1:21-28)*, an incident we looked at in chapter 14. Not something you'd be likely to forget in a hurry.

Until now, Jesus has been lamenting the lack of faith among the Jews *(Luke 7:9)*. Here at last, though from a most unexpected source, is someone from among His own people who has no doubt that Jesus is able to perform a miracle and heal his daughter. Even though Jesus probably has a strong case for regarding this synagogue ruler as an enemy, Pharisee that he is, He doesn't reject him and send him packing. His response to Jairus's faith is immediate. He willingly goes with him, accompanied, not surprisingly, by *'a large crowd'* who *'pressed around him' (Mark 5:24)*.

Delay on the way

How must Jairus have felt when Jesus stopped to deal with the sick woman on the way? *(25-34)*. Frustration seems an inadequate word to describe the emotions he must have been experiencing. His daughter was dying; every second was vital; and the answer to his prayers was standing there asking, 'Who touched my clothes?', and refusing to take another step until the matter is sorted out. Or maybe I do Jairus an injustice. Perhaps he had such faith in Jesus that getting home as quickly as possible was of no concern to him whatever.

And then Jairus sees some men he recognizes coming from the direction of his house, and he knows it's bad news. And he's right. These men certainly don't spare his feelings as they announce in a cold, matter-of-fact way: '"Your daughter is dead. . . .Why bother the teacher any more?"' (35b). It's that sort of moment when your heart sinks, and you have that awful feeling in the pit of your stomach. The bottom has just fallen out of his world, and he has difficulty holding back his emotions.

Bother to bother

Jesus knows exactly how Jairus is feeling and what is going through his mind. He ignores what the messengers have said, and for the first time He speaks directly to Jairus, right into the depths of his despair. And what wonderful yet challenging words they are: 'Don't be afraid; just believe, and she will be healed' (Luke 8:50). The Amplified Bible renders this: 'Do not be seized with alarm or struck with fear; simply believe [in Me as able to do this], and she shall be made well'. Once again, we see how crucial it is for us to allow faith to conquer fear, and to believe that God is able to do the impossible. The apostle Paul tells us that God 'is able to do immeasurably more than all we ask or imagine' (Ephesians 3:20).

It's so easy in times of deep despair or great difficulty to adopt the human perspective of the messengers, and come to the conclusion that it's not worth bothering God about the situation. But God wants us to bother Him. It shows we have the faith to believe He is able to do something about this apparently impossible situation: and that He not only can, but will.

I remember once being rather taken aback when a colleague at school described me as a 'God-botherer' when she discovered that I prayed regularly. It gave me a splendid opportunity to explain that God wasn't at all bothered that I bothered Him in this way. In fact, He wishes that more of us could be bothered to bother Him, preferably on a regular basis.

The inner circle

Interestingly, Jesus doesn't seem to wait for any confirmation from Jairus that his faith is undiminished, even though He has now required him to move from a position of believing the difficult to believing the impossible. He doesn't engage him in conversation, as He did the father of the boy with the evil spirit [see chapter 16], in order to determine the depth of his faith. He just sets off for Jairus's house.

Luke tells us that when He got there, *'he did not let anyone go in with him except Peter, John and James, and the child's father and mother' (8:51).* Jesus allowed only these three from among the twelve disciples to be present with Him on three particular occasions. The other two are the Transfiguration of Jesus *(Mark 9:2)*, and the agony of Jesus in the Garden of Gethsemane prior to His arrest *(Mark 14:33)*. The three of them seem to have had a particularly close relationship with Jesus, and were privileged to experience at first hand His power over death, His divinity, and His humanity. Peter and John went on to be in the forefront of the miraculous in the Early Church, *(Acts 3-5, 8:14-25)*, while James was one of its first martyrs *(Acts 12:1, 2)*.

Rent-a-mourner

It is very unlikely that the widow of Nain could have afforded to hire professional mourners [chapter 17], but Jairus's household certainly could, and had gone ahead and done so already *(Mark 5:38)*.

Jesus tells the mourners quite clearly that *'"The child is not dead but asleep"' (39b)*. Jesus habitually referred to death as a sleep *(John 11:11-14)*. The reaction of the mourners tells its own story *(Mark 5:40a)*. *Luke* makes it even more explicit *(8:53)*. They knew death when they saw it! Having ushered the mourners outside, the six of them proceed to where the dead girl lies.

Getting to grips

I try to picture this moving scene. Jairus and his wife, clinging to each other for mutual comfort and support, tears running down their cheeks, scarcely daring to breathe. Their beloved daughter, their only child, lying motionless. Peter, John and James hovering in the background, perhaps remembering what has happened recently on the road outside Nain. Jesus, approaching the bed upon which rests the body of the girl. He bends over the still figure, extends His arm towards her, and takes her hand in His. Gently, but, as The Amplified Bible puts it: *'Gripping her [firmly] by the hand' (Mark 5:41a)*, He speaks these words to her: *'"Talitha cumi"' (41b)*.

These were the actual Aramaic words that Jesus used. The word translated by Mark as *'little girl'* has a very affectionate tone to it, rather like calling a child a 'lamb'. The reason Mark gives a translation in his account is because the majority of his readers would have been unfamiliar with this Palestinian dialect, which apparently Jesus used most of the time. The phrase *'get up' (41c)* actually means 'Arise from the sleep of death!', which is how The Amplified Bible renders it. Once again, Jesus just speaks the word, and even death has to release its grip.

The girl responds to this command with astonishing alacrity. Mark is again able to use one of his favourite words as he tells us: *'Immediately the girl stood up and walked around' (42a)*.

Practical and impractical

But before the inevitable family celebrations begin, Jesus has a couple of things to say to the astonished parents. In fact, *Mark* describes what Jesus said as being *'strict orders' (43a)*.

Firstly, they are *'not to let anyone know about this' (43a)*. This is all to do with the 'Messianic Secret' that we looked at in chapter 6, although such a command does seem to be impractical to say the least. The second command is surprisingly practical: *'give her something to eat' (43b)*. Jesus is concerned for the girl's physical welfare. He knows she hasn't had a meal for some time, and will therefore be feeling very weak. Perhaps He mentions it, because in the euphoria of the moment such practical considerations may be overlooked by her parents. And it's another lovely example of Jesus' care for and attention to the detail of our lives.

CHAPTER NINETEEN

LAZARUS LIVES
[Jesus raises Lazarus from the dead]
John 11:1-53

The family at Bethany

We come now to what is undoubtedly the most spectacular of the three demonstrations of Jesus' power over death: as if the other two weren't dramatic enough!

Jesus receives word that Lazarus is sick *(3)*. Lazarus has two sisters, Martha and Mary, and the three of them live in Bethany *(1)*, a village situated about two miles east of Jerusalem. From the wording of the message *(3)* it is clear that Jesus has become very great friends with the three of them. Apparently, whenever Jesus was in the vicinity of Jerusalem, He used to stay at their house *(Mark 11:11)*. Indeed, Luke tells us about one of Jesus' visits there *(Luke 10:38-42)*. Lazarus is not mentioned, but what occurred gives us a fascinating insight – which is reflected in this incident – into the different personalities of the two sisters.

Chalk and cheese

Martha may have been the eldest of the three. If we accept this supposition, it helps explain why she was used to taking charge and being in control. She was very hospitable, well organized, eager to please, and keen to do the right thing. She took a pride in her home, her cooking, and her practical service to her guests.

Mary was somewhat different. For her, hospitality was more about spending time with the guest rather than making sure everything was just right for him. To Mary, conversation was more important than the smooth running of the home. She was a listener, who thought deeply before she spoke or acted. When she did do something, it was often profound: for example, her anointing of Jesus' feet showed an understanding of His death that seemed to have escaped the other disciples *(John 12:1-8)*. This was so unlike Martha, who couldn't help coming out with her thoughts and feelings on the spur of the moment.

It's not difficult to see how Mary's attitude would have irritated Martha, and vice versa. But, complementing each other as they did, they made a very effective team, though Jesus had lessons to teach them both.

Knitting without the needles

It seems to me that the family of the church experiences the same tensions as those evident in this family. People of different abilities, attitudes, opinions, expectations, personalities, and ways of operating, all interacting simultaneously. No wonder there are problems at times.

How important it is that we seek to work as a team under the direction of the Holy Spirit, who will knit us together into an effective, cohesive unit that can serve the Lord Jesus Christ in the Bethany in which He has placed us. This will happen only as we value one another, as we recognize and seek to develop one another's ministries, and as we actively support and encourage one another.

However, the Spirit's process of knitting us together can be severely hampered by the needle of wrong attitudes towards one another within the family of the church. The result is that the pattern which God has specifically designed for us can never be realized, and consequently we are nowhere near as effective and cohesive a unit as He brought us together to be.

The hardest of times

Jesus' response to receiving the news of His friend Lazarus' illness is surprising to say the least. First of all, there is what He says *(4)*. From His words, we can see that Jesus knows that

Lazarus is going to die, but He also knows that his death will not be the end of the matter. It is going to be the opportunity for God to show His glory, and for Jesus Himself to be glorified through it. This will happen in two ways. The miracle He will perform will show the glory and power of God in Jesus; and it will help to set in motion the events that will lead to the cross, where Jesus will ultimately show the glory and power of God in His victory over sin and death and hell.

Secondly, there is what Jesus does: or rather, what He does not do. Having reiterated Jesus' deep love for this family *(5)*, John then tells us that he *'stayed where he was two more days' (6b)*. So clearly He didn't do this because He didn't care. There was a divine purpose to all this that for the moment was beyond human understanding.

There may be times when we find something similar, although perhaps not nearly as drastic, happening to us. Times when, like Martha, we can't see any possible reason for God's not responding to our prayers. Times when, like these two sisters, we are oblivious to the fact that God is working out His purposes in our situation in a way that we wouldn't be able to comprehend, even if He told us.

Love undiminished

What a test this is of the sisters' love for Jesus. They expect Him to come at once, but He doesn't. They must have sat down together and discussed why this might be, without coming up with any satisfactory answers as to why the one who said He loved them had failed to respond by coming and healing Lazarus, as no doubt He could have done, thus leaving them weeping and mourning the death of their beloved brother. None of it made any sense. And yet, although Martha can't resist making a comment to Jesus on the subject when He does finally appear on the scene, as does Mary a little later, there is no hint whatever of a lessening of their love for Him: it remains undiminished.

This raises another uncomfortable question for us. Does our

love for God pass this severest of tests, or are we guilty of being the sort of people whose love for God depends on what He does for us? Or can we honestly say that if God never answers another one of our prayers it will make absolutely no difference at all to our wholehearted love for Him: the One who loved *us* so wholeheartedly that He sacrificed Himself on the cross that we might experience such love?

Divine compliment

It seems to me that Jesus was so certain of the love of Martha and Mary, so sure it wouldn't falter or melt away when He didn't come and Lazarus died, that He knew He could put them through such a trial as this. What a compliment they were being paid by God Himself, although I'm sure they didn't appreciate it at the time.

And, because the sisters' love was steadfast, enduring and undiminished, they were going to see the power and glory of God made manifest in their lives in a way that they could never have dreamt of. True, their friends and the others present would see it too, but it would affect Martha and Mary personally, and make a dramatic impact on their lives, not to mention on their level of faith.

The cost of obedience

Jesus decides that the time has now come to make the journey to Bethany, which, like Jerusalem, lies in the province of Judea *(7)*. The disciples are not happy about this, and with good reason *(8)*. Jesus is literally going to be risking life and limb if He goes back to Judea. At the moment, He is some miles away to the east of the River Jordan in the district of Perea.

Yet, while the disciples are thinking of His safety, Jesus is thinking solely of His work in obedience to His Father's will. Being obedient means that we are walking in the light *(9)*. Disobedience to God means that we are walking in the dark, without the light of God shining in our lives; and that is the way of disaster *(10)*.

Obedience means that we are giving up any notion of doing things our way any more. We are submitting ourselves to the Lordship of Christ in our lives, becoming His servants. The apostle Paul uses the picture of slavery to describe what is required of us *(Romans 6:15-23)*. Doing what God wants us to do can be costly and demand sacrifices on our part. That's why Jesus advises us to weigh up carefully the implications of becoming His disciples before making the decision *(Luke 14:25-33)*.

For Jesus, His obedience to the Father required Him to pay the ultimate price and to sacrifice His life that the world might be saved *(Philippians 2:8b)*. For us, it is unlikely to mean death: but it does mean dying to ourselves, following Jesus *(Mark 8:34)*, and showing our love for Him by obeying His commands *(John 14:15)*.

Puzzling words

Jesus then tries to explain to the disciples that He is going to bring Lazarus back to life *(11)*, but they misunderstand, and think that Jesus is just going to heal him *(12)*. This is why Jesus then categorically states that *'"Lazarus is dead"' (14)*, so there can be no doubt in their minds that what they are about to witness is not a miracle of healing, but a demonstration of the power of Jesus over death itself.

Jesus then goes on to say something that must have puzzled the disciples greatly: *'and for your sake I am glad I was not there' (15a)*. What He means is that if He had been there during Lazarus' last hours, Jesus would have healed him, and thus prevented him from dying. This in turn would have meant that the disciples would not have been able to see the demonstration of the power and glory of God that they were about to witness. And this was all going to happen, Jesus told His disciples, *'"so that you may believe"' (15b)*. The bringing of the disciples to faith in Him was a vital part of their training; so much so, that here it seemed almost to supersede the needs of Martha and Mary.

The road to death

And with these words ringing in the men's ears, Jesus announces that it is time to go to Lazarus *(15c)*. This only serves to rekindle the fears which the disciples expressed previously to Jesus *(8)*, but, perhaps surprisingly, it is Thomas who articulates what they all must be feeling *(16)*. Thomas, who is to become a byword for doubting, here shows great courage and loyalty. He leads them down the road which they are all expecting will lead to death.

By the time Jesus and His disciples arrive in Bethany, *'Lazarus had already been in the tomb for four days' (17b)*. Apparently, many Jews believed that the soul of the deceased lingered near the body for three days following the death, in the hope of returning to it. Now that four days had passed, all hope was gone. Lazarus was definitely and irrevocably dead; it was beyond doubt. The Jewish traditions surrounding burial, with or without hired mourners, had been and were still being observed. This meant there were still a lot of people around visiting Martha and Mary to comfort them; most of them had come from Jerusalem *(18, 19)*. This shows the high regard in which the family was held.

Statements

On hearing that Jesus is approaching the village, the two sisters react completely differently, but in the way we might expect from what we already know of them. Martha bustles off to meet Jesus, whereas Mary stays at home *(20)*. Martha has one or two things to say, whereas Mary is too full of grief to stir herself.

Martha gets straight to the point the moment she meets Jesus. There follows a conversation between the two of them, the content of which she could never have imagined. *'"Lord," Martha said to Jesus, "if you had been here, my brother would not have died"' (21)*. We can only speculate as to the tone of voice in which she delivered these words, but it is hard to imagine that there was not a touch of regret, even mild reproach, in there somewhere.

But this statement of fact is followed by a tremendous statement of faith: ' *"But I know that even now God will give you whatever you ask"' (22)*. What did Martha have in mind when she said this? Was it just a vague faith statement made in hope? Was it a statement made just because she thought that was the sort of thing that Jesus would want to hear? Or did she really have the faith to believe in a resurrection from the dead? Maybe she and Mary had reminded each other of the two previous occasions when Jesus had brought people back to life, and this is what Martha was reflecting here in this specific faith statement.

Superhighway

Jesus reminds Martha of the Jewish hope of the resurrection *(23)*. Martha thinks that the Day of Resurrection lies a long way into the future *(24)*, but Jesus stuns her and everyone else around Him with these amazing words: ' *"I am the resurrection and the life. He who believes in me will live, even though he dies; and whoever lives and believes in me will never die"' (25a)*. Jesus has the power to conquer death, and the power to give life: not only natural life, but eternal life.

When we put our belief and trust in Jesus, we receive the gift of eternal life *(John 3:16)*; so even though we die, eternal life is still in our future. Death is not a dead end. There *is* life after life! *(1 Thessalonians 4:16; Luke 23:43; 2 Corinthians 5:8; Philippians 1:23)*. And if we are still alive when He returns, then we shall indeed 'never die', because we shall be *'caught up . . . to meet the Lord in the air. And so we will be with the Lord forever'* *(1 Thessalonians 4:17)*. What a glorious future awaits us!

Pivotal moment

All that has happened so far has been leading up to this moment when Jesus makes His 'I am' declaration: one of seven recorded in this gospel *(6:35; 8:12; 10:7; 10:11; 11:25; 14:6; 15:1)*. What Jesus has said in word, He is about to carry out in deed. But before He does so, He has a critical question for Martha:

'"*Do you believe this?*"' *(26b)*. Does she have the faith to believe the truth of what Jesus has just said?

Faced with the enormity of such a statement, Martha testifies to her faith and belief in Jesus as the Messiah and the Son of God *(27)*. Though she may not understand all the ramifications of resurrection and eternal life, she does understand that Jesus is the Son of God, and that is enough. Her statement of faith is of great significance as far as John is concerned, and it is exactly the same response that Jesus requires of us. Making it is undoubtedly the pivotal moment in our lives.

Jesus then presumably asks after Mary, because Martha goes back to fetch her *(28-30)*. Their Jewish visitors who had come to mourn with them accompany Mary, assuming she's going to the tomb *(31)*. When Mary meets Jesus, we see again the contrast between the two sisters. Mary says exactly the same words as her sister has previously voiced *(21, 32)*, which suggests they have discussed Jesus' lack of response to their message many times. But, whereas Martha had stood there and spoken to Jesus face to face, Mary is on her knees and can't stop weeping *(32, 33a)*. This same conviction that the sisters express is echoed by some of the mourners *(37)*, who were obviously present when Jesus healed the man born blind *(9:1-7)*, which we looked at in chapter 10.

Humanity displayed

Now we come to one of the two most vivid portrayals of the humanity of Jesus to be found in the gospels *(33-36)*. The other one is in the Garden of Gethsemane *(Luke 22:39-44)*. Here we see a God who empathizes with us and is deeply moved by our situation *(33, 34)*, who weeps with us and cares deeply about us *(35, 36)*. What an encouragement this is to us. God loves us so much that He is prepared to involve Himself with us in our daily lives. He understands our deepest emotions, because He has experienced them for Himself. So when we pray, we are not coming to a God who hasn't got a clue about how we're feeling. He knows. He cares. He understands. And His compassion never fails.

This was completely different from the Greek concept of God which was around at that time. This portrayed a God with no feelings or emotions, who would certainly not involve Himself with the nitty-gritty of the daily life and problems of human beings.

Here, for all to see, was Jesus displaying the true nature of God. He could have gone straight to the tomb and performed the miracle as soon as Mary had appeared. But He didn't. He wanted to reveal the compassionate heart of God to all those who were there. This serves to emphasize how important it is to God that we grasp the truth of the fact that He understands us and wants to be involved with us.

Divinity displayed

- *Consequences*

Having shown His humanity in such a vivid way, Jesus now proceeds to affirm His divinity in an even more dramatic display.

In those days, tombs were usually caves cut into the limestone hillsides. You could walk into and around them in an upright position, and several bodies were normally placed in one tomb. A large stone or rock was positioned across the entrance *(38)*. Jesus gives the command for this to be removed *(39a)*. Martha, practical to the last, is concerned about the unpleasant consequences of such an action *(39b)*. I can just imagine her raising her hand up to her nose as she speaks of the *'bad odour'*!

And we have to face up to the possibility that once God becomes involved in a situation and begins to act, there will more than likely be consequences and implications that might not quite accord with our sensibilities or expectations. Ignoring her protest, Jesus turns to the disciples, and reminds them of their conversation back in Perea *(4, 14, 15, 40)*.

- *The moving process*

I like to think that it is actually the disciples themselves who *'took away the stone' (41a)*. Having perhaps hesitated when first told to do so *(39a)*, as soon as Jesus reminds them that they are about to witness a display of the glory of God, they respond immediately. They demonstrate their belief in what Jesus has said by moving the stone, which is the barrier to this miracle's taking place.

There may be a barrier in our own lives, such as unbelief or doubt, which needs to be moved so that we can experience the blessing of God flowing through us and His glory being revealed to us. The stone can be seen as being symbolic of such a barrier, not only in our own lives but in the lives of those disciples. Their struggle to move the stone speaks of their inner struggle to deal with their own unbelief: a struggle that we all experience at times. But, once the barrier has been removed, God is able to act.

• *Thanks in anticipation*

Now everything is ready, Jesus prays out loud for the benefit of the assembled crowd *(41b, 42)*. It is interesting that Jesus gives thanks to the Father for hearing Him before there is any evidence that anything has happened.

This is an encouragement to us to give God thanks in anticipation of what He is going to do in response to our prayers before they have actually been answered. This is an expression of our complete faith, belief and trust in God. As the writer to the Hebrews put it: *'Now faith is being sure of what we hope for and certain of what we do not see' (Hebrews 11:1)*. It was just this sort of prayer that James had in mind when he wrote his epistle *(James 5:15)*.

'"Come out!"'

I try to picture the scene. Jesus, with Martha and Mary at His side, facing the tomb; the stone rolled away to one side, where the disciples are standing; the crowd of mourners, swollen by curious villagers, form a semi-circle behind Jesus. There is a short, tense silence. Jesus prays to the Father. The tension builds. Jesus then shouts loudly: *'"Lazarus, come out!"' (43)*.

All eyes are fixed on the entrance to the tomb. How long it

takes before Lazarus actually appears we are not told. Gasps of amazement and cries of disbelief suddenly fill the air as a figure, slowly and with some difficulty, emerges from the darkness of the tomb, *'his hands and feet wrapped with strips of linen, and a cloth around his face' (44a)*.

Martha, for once, seems lost for words. Along with her wide-eyed sister, she is rooted to the spot, probably with her mouth wide open, but with nothing coming out. They are both vaguely aware of Jesus saying: *'"Take off the grave clothes and let him go"' (44b)*. Whom Jesus actually says this to, we are not told. Is it the disciples who go to his assistance? Or is it Martha and Mary who joyfully fly to his aid? Whoever it is, Lazarus is released, given new life and restored to his family.

Alive to God

What a poignant picture this is of each one of us. We were once sinful, making us dead to God. But, having responded to His personal call, we have now been released from the bondage of our sin, given new life in Christ, and had our family relationship with God our Father restored.

The apostle Paul describes what has happened to us in these words: *'When you were dead in your sins . . . God made you alive' (Colossians 2:13)*. As a result of this, he says: *'Count yourselves dead to sin but alive to God in Christ Jesus. Therefore do not let sin reign in your mortal body so that you obey its evil desires. Do not offer the parts of your body to sin, as instruments of wickedness, but rather offer yourselves to God, as those who have been brought from death to life; and offer the parts of your body to him as instruments of righteousness' (Romans 6:11-13)*. In other words, we have been made alive to God, not simply for our own benefit but for the express purpose of serving Him *(Romans 6:22a; Hebrews 9:14c)*.

Sad postscript

There is a sad note to all this: and that is the fact that, even when confronted with such a display of Jesus' divinity, many still refused to believe. Rather, they went off to tell the

Pharisees, who *'from that day on . . . plotted to take his life'* (53). Thus, restoring Lazarus to life becomes the immediate cause of Jesus' own death, as of course He knew it would be.

At those times when I'm trying my best to witness and share my faith, with little apparent success, I remind myself that not only didn't people believe when they saw such a demonstration as this, but they didn't even believe when they saw and met the risen Christ Himself *(Matthew 28:17)*.

Four-shadowing

This incident is a remarkable foreshadowing of what was to happen shortly afterwards to Jesus Himself. He would be placed in a tomb; the stone of that tomb would be moved; His burial clothes would be remarked on; He would be raised from the dead. Perhaps Jesus was *'deeply moved'* as He *'came to the tomb'* (38a) for more than the obvious reasons.

• The tomb

These four similarities or comparisons also provide us with a series of interesting contrasts. Firstly, the tomb in which Jesus was placed was brand new *(Matthew 27:60)*; His was the first body to be laid in it *(Luke 23:53)*, and, by implication, His was the only body in there. When Jesus summoned Lazarus from the tomb, He had to call him specifically by name, otherwise, presumably all the other bodies in that tomb would have come back to life!

• The stone

Secondly, no people were required to move the stone at Jesus' tomb; that was done by an angel *(Matthew 28:2)*. In the case of Lazarus, the stone was moved so he could get out. In the case of Jesus, the stone wasn't rolled back so that He could get out; it was moved so that the women, and later the other disciples who came, could get in to see what had happened.

- *The clothes*

Thirdly, Lazarus came out still wearing his burial clothes, and had to be released from them by other people. Jesus did not need to be released from His burial clothes by anyone. The ones He had been wrapped in were left behind in the tomb, folded up *(Luke 24:12b; John 20:6b, 7)*.

- *The raising*

Fourthly, Lazarus, having been raised from the dead, dies again. Jesus, having been raised from the dead, dies no more. He is *'alive for ever and ever' (Revelation 1:18a)*. Which reminds me of those wonderful, reassuring words of Jesus: *'"Because I live, you also will live"' (John 14:19b)*.

Someone once wrote these telling words:

> *'Man can give medicine when sickness comes,*
> *Food when hunger comes,*
> *Help when weakness comes,*
> *Love when loneliness comes.*
> *But when death comes, man can give*
> *Only sympathy, only compassion,*
> *Never the gift of life.*
> *Only God can do that.'*

And that is one of the greatest miracles of all.

APPENDIX 1

MIRACLES IN PROBABLE CHRONOLOGICAL ORDER

		Chapter
Water into wine	*John 2:1-11*	1
Man with an evil spirit	*Mark 1:21-28; Luke 4:31-37*	14
Catch of fish	*Luke 5:4-11*	2
A leprosy sufferer	*Matthew 8:2-4; Mark 1:40-45; Luke 5:12-14*	6
A paralysed man	*Matthew 9:2-8; Mark 2:1-12; Luke 5:18-26*	7
Man with a shrivelled hand	*Mark 3:1-6; Luke 6:6-11*	11
Centurion's servant	*Matthew 8:5-13; Luke 7:1-10*	12
Widow of Nain's son	*Luke 7:11-17*	17
Calming the storm	*Matthew 8:23-27; Mark 4:35-41; Luke 8:22-25*	3
Gerasene demoniac	*Mark 5:1-20; Luke 8:26-37*	15
A sick woman	*Matthew 9:20-22; Mark 5:24-34; Luke 8:42-44*	8
Jairus's daughter	*Matthew 9:18-19, 23-26; Mark 5:21-24, 35-43; Luke 8:41, 42, 49-56*	18
Feeding the 5,000	*Matthew 14:13-21; Mark 6:30-44; Luke 9:10-17; John 6:1-13*	4
Walking on the water	*Matthew 14:22, 23; Mark 6:45-52; John 6:16-21*	5
Canaanite woman's daughter	*Matthew 15:21-28; Mark 7:24-30*	13
Boy with an evil spirit	*Matthew 17:14-20; Mark 9:14-29; Luke 9:37-43*	16
A crippled woman	*Luke 13:10-17*	11
Blind Bartimaeus	*Mark 10:46-52; Luke 18:35-43*	9
A man born blind	*John 9:1-41*	10
The raising of Lazarus	*John 11:1-53*	19

APPENDIX 2

REFERENCES QUOTED OR SUGGESTED FOR FURTHER STUDY

		Page			Page
Genesis	1, 3	104, 105	Matthew	17	41
Exodus	3:14	55		22:1-14	14
	20	35, 41		23:1-36	93
	20:8-11	103		23:25-28	108
	32-33:6	144		24:3	15
Leviticus	11:7	135		25:1-13	14
	13, 14	62		25:41	127
	14:1-32	65		27:60	172
	15:25-33	79		28:2	172
	24:16	73		28:16-20	121
	25:35-38	84		28:17	172
Deuteronomy	8:3	48		28:18-20	139
Joshua	6	83		28:19, 20	114
	7:19, 20	95	Mark	1:13, 15	123
1 Kings	17:17-24	153		1:20	26
	18	41		1:30	15
2 Kings	4:18-37	153		3:15	143
	5:1-14	66		6:6	114
Job	23:10	151		6:13	143
Psalm	1:1-3	66		6:35, 36	15
	89:9	33		7:20-23	117
	107:28, 29	33		8:1-13	48
	139:2	101		8:22-25	91
Ecclesiastes	11:1	48		8:34	89, 165
Isaiah	53:5	105		9	41
	61:10	137		9:2	159
	64:6	137		9:28	15
Jeremiah	5:23	144		10:51	15
	31:13	151		11:11	161
Daniel	3:26	133		11:22, 23	10
	7:13, 14	74		12:13	104
Habakkuk	3:17, 18	121		14:33	159
Matthew	2:1	83		14:61-64	73
	4:1-4	48		14:62	74
	4:25	137		16:17, 18	127
	6:8	15	Luke	1:37	152
	6:33	26		4:1-13, 14	123
	7:7	120		4:18	132
	8:25	15		4:18, 19	123
	10:19, 20	140		4:28-30	124
	12:22-28	126		7:9	157
	12:43-45	129		7:18-23	113
	15:18-20	117		9	41
	15:32-39	48		9:2, 6	37
	16:15-18	96		9:38	15